SHOTS FROM THE FRONT

ALSO BY RICHARD HOLMES

In order of publication

SHOTS FROM THE FRONT

The British Soldier 1914–18

RICHARD HOLMES

Harper
Press

ɔor's deepest respect for
tion that endured

HarperPress
An imprint of HarperCollins*Publishers*
77–85 Fulham Palace Road,
Hammersmith, London W6 8JB
www.harpercollins.com

Published by HarperPress in 2008

A catalogue record for this book is
available from the British Library

ISBN 13 978-0-00-727548-9
ISBN 10 0-00-727548-X

Set in Stempel Garamond

Designed by Terence Caven

Printed and bound in Italy by
Rotolito Lombarda

Contents

Author's Note

This book is about soldiers. Most soldiers who served in the British Army during the First World War were privates, though some arms of the service had their own terminology for this rank. In rifle regiments privates were called riflemen; they were troopers in the Household Cavalry (though privates in line cavalry and yeomanry till 1922), gunners or drivers in the Royal Artillery, sappers in the Royal Engineers, and drivers in the Army Service Corps. Private soldiers in the five regiments of foot guards – Grenadier, Coldstream, Scots, Irish and Welsh (the latter raised in 1915) – were called privates during the war, but on the headstones of those killed the War Graves Commission has awarded them the post-war title of guardsman. Non-commissioned officers began with junior NCOs, the single-stripe lance corporal and the two-stripe corporal. At that time the Royal Artillery retained the rank of corporal, its two-stripe rank which was senior to the traditional artillery rank of bombardier.

Some units had the intermediate three-stripe rank of lance sergeant, ranking junior to the senior NCOs proper, the sergeant and the staff sergeant (known as colour sergeant in the infantry), whose three stripes were topped by a crown. There were two grades of warrant officer, both of which covered a variety of appointments. Warrant Officers Class 2, with a crown on their cuff, were company sergeant majors in the infantry, squadron sergeant majors in the cavalry, and so on. The best-known (though not always best-loved) Warrant Officers Class 1 were regimental sergeant majors, and the most senior held the distinctive title of conductor in the Army Ordnance Corps.

Warrant officers were so called because they held a warrant from the Army Council, the body created in 1904 to implement the prerogative powers of the crown in relation to the army, and could be deprived of it only by sentence of court-martial.

All non-commissioned personnel ('other ranks') received numbers on enlistment. These were an essential means of distinguishing one soldier from another in some regiments: Jones *tout court* would mean little in a battalion of Royal Welch Fusiliers, but everyone would know who 'Jones Two-Six' (the last two digits of his number) was. During the First World War numbers were regimental, and if a man was posted from one regiment to another he would receive a new one. Some regiments applied an 'S' prefix to the numbers of men joining their wartime-raised 'Service' battalions. The Territorials made matters even more difficult by carrying out a comprehensive renumbering in 1917.

Officers held the King's commission. The one-pip second lieutenant and the two-pip lieutenant were known as subalterns. Captains sported three pips, majors a crown, lieutenant colonels crown and pip, and full colonels (rare beasts in 1914–18) two pips and a crown. Brigadier generals wore crossed sword and baton on their shoulder, major generals added a single pip, lieutenant generals a crown, and full generals both crown and pip. Field marshals wore crossed batons wreathed in laurel. A commanding officer (CO by abbreviation) was the lieutenant colonel commanding a unit like an infantry battalion. A sub-unit, such as an infantry company, cavalry squadron or artillery battery, had as its officer commanding (OC) generally a captain in the infantry and a major in the cavalry or artillery. Adjutants, usually captains, were the personal staff officers of COs.

Rank could be permanent, held until retirement (for officers) or discharge (for soldiers) unless lost as a result of due process. Most wartime commissions were temporary, and many wartime promotions gave only acting rank, which would evaporate the moment the appointment to which it attached was relinquished. Officers often held acting rank well in advance of their substantive wartime rank. Lieutenant Colonel J.N. Marshall, killed winning the Victoria Cross in the closing stages of the war, was a substantive lieutenant, and the notoriously insubordinate and foul-tempered Keppel Bethell, appointed to command the 66th Division as a temporary major general in 1918 at the age of thirty-five, was a substantive captain at the time. Officers could be awarded brevet rank, a reward for brave or distinguished service, and this gave them rank in the army, though not in their own regiments, so conferred status without giving a right to specific employment.

During the First World War the Royal Regiment of Artillery comprised a mounted branch, the Royal Field and Royal Horse Artillery, and a dismounted branch, the Royal Garrison Artillery. Artillery batteries – for example 7th Siege Battery Royal Garrison Artillery, C Battery Royal Horse Artillery, or 12th Battery Royal Field Artillery – had a distinctive and lasting identity in a way that infantry companies did not. Batteries were combined (with an ammunition column added) into artillery brigades. An artillery brigade was, like an infantry battalion, a lieutenant colonel's command.

Brigades, divisions, corps and armies were called formations, and their commanders were styled General Officers Commanding, or GOCs. Formation establishments changed a good deal as the war went on. Until the winter of 1917, when shortage of manpower brought the number down to three, there were four battalions in each brigade. There were generally three brigades in a division, a major general's command. This was the first all-arms formation, for in 1914 it included three brigades of field artillery and a heavy battery under a brigadier general known as the Commander Royal Artillery or CRA, field companies Royal Engineers under a colonel styled as the Commander Royal Engineers or CRE, three field ambulances (each a lieutenant colonel's command) as well as a company of the Royal Engineers Signal Service, its own logistic unit (the 'divisional train') and a cavalry squadron for reconnaissance, route-signing and message-carrying. Divisions gained added resources as the war went on. Some divisions had titles denoting their origin, like the Territorial 51st (Highland) Division or the New Army 16th (Irish) Division, although by 1918 manpower pressures forced Highlanders onto English county regiments and Brummies into the Black Watch.

The corps, commanded by a lieutenant general and defined by a Roman numeral, usually contained three divisions, which might be switched between different corps as the situation evolved, and as the war went on it included an increasing number of 'corps troops' like heavy guns, machine-gun battalions and counter-battery staff, which gave it a significant battle-shaping capacity in its own right. Armies were commanded by generals. There were eventually five on the Western Front, and they varied in size even more radically than the corps that made them up. Fifth Army, Field Marshal Haig's chosen instrument at the start of the third battle of Ypres in 1917, was stuffed full of corps at the same time that Third Army, out of the line, was so under-resourced that its commander scarcely knew how to fill his day. As corps contained their own assets apart from their divisions, so too 'army troops' enabled army commanders to do their own shaping of the battle by committing these resources to key points.

Just as most soldiers were privates, most privates served in the infantry. The great bulk of infantry formed the regiments of the line, organised in 1881 into county regiments by the combination of the old numbered line regiments: for instance, the 37th and 67th Regiments, both with a Hampshire affiliation, became the Hampshire Regiment. Most regiments had two regular battalions, a Special Reserve battalion intended to produce reinforcements for the regulars on mobilisation, and a number of part-time Territorial battalions, their officers and men not initially obliged to serve abroad unless they volunteered to do so. Extra battalions were raised by Lord Kitchener's appeal for volunteers in 1914. These 'New Army' units were numbered after the Territorial battalions of their regiments, and properly took the bracketed title '(Service)' after their number. Many had informal titles too, like the Accrington Pals for 11th East Yorkshire and the Sheffield City Battalion for 12th York and Lancaster.

The British Official History abbreviates by styling 1st Battalion the Queen's Royal West Surrey Regiment as 1/Queen's, and I follow the same practice here. On mobilisation Territorial battalions split into first-line units, whose men were fit and had volunteered for foreign service, and second- and later third- and sometimes fourth-line battalions too. The first-line battalion formed from 4/Queen's was 1/4th Queen's, its second-line battalion 2/4th Queen's, and so on. In August 1914 a battalion might number 1,000 men and thirty officers, but for much of the war it was more likely to contain 500–700 men and something over twenty officers. Its four companies had four platoons apiece, each commanded by a subaltern with a sergeant at his elbow, and containing four sections (perhaps five men when times were hard, and eight when they were good), each under a corporal.

This book is not much concerned with the great and the good, but is greatly preoccupied with the folk with broken fingernails, stubbly chins and lousy shirts who made up the real strength of an army built to endure. There is just one brigadier general in its pages (a brave man going forward on foot), but an awful lot of corporals.

Prologue

Over my career as a military historian I have spent longer on the Western Front than any wartime combatant. When I first stood under the Menin Gate, listening to the buglers of the Ypres fire brigade sound the Last Post, the veterans around me were not much older then than I am now, and I was then closer to Passchendaele than I now am to D-Day. I was just older than the youngest soldiers to be killed in the war – Private John Condon of the Royal Irish, who died at the age of fourteen, and Private Valentine Joe Strudwick of the Rifle Brigade, who was fifteen. My father died when I was eighteen, long before I had any career in view, and amongst his possessions I found snapshots he had taken in northern France and Belgium in 1929. Among them is one of John Condon's grave, in Fig. 1. The print is old and its framing far from perfect, but I include it here because it sends a sharp jolt of connectivity across the years.

I am still younger than the oldest military victim of the war, Lieutenant Henry Webber of the South Lancashire, killed on the Somme at sixty-eight. Webber, a well-to-do widower from Horley in Surrey, had been a member of the London Stock Exchange for over forty years, and had sufficient influence to secure himself a commission, though he was well over-age. The commanding officer of 7/South Lancashire sensibly made him the transport officer, so that he would be back in the transport lines with his horses and wagons when the battalion was in the trenches. No photograph of him seems to have survived, but for an image of tired transport men on the Somme we

Fig. 1
(opposite)

Fig. 2   cannot do better than Fig. 2, which shows a driver of the transport section of a Devon battalion using one of his horses as a pillow. Not long before Henry Webber was killed he wrote:

> Fifty-one years ago I got my colours in the eleven, and last week fifty-one years ago I was bowling against the Old Boys, and looking on some of them as 'sitters' and in 'the sere and yellow leaf,' and here I am a Lieutenant in His Majesty's Army, having to salute three sons if I meet them out here, a Colonel and two Majors . . . I am so far extraordinarily fit and well, and though when I tell you that for four consecutive days I was either on my feet or in the saddle for twenty-one hours out of the twenty-four you will see that there is a bit of work to it.
>
> Our boys were simply splendid and now, after a rest, they are as keen as – well, as a schoolboy to be put on to bowl.

The battalion was part of 19th (Western) Division, in reserve at the start of the Somme but it was soon committed and helped take La Boisselle on 2–5 July.

Shortly afterwards German artillery fire caught its transport lines, and Webber was mortally wounded, dying on 21 July. His eldest son, Norman William 'Squib' Webber, finished the war as Brigadier General, General Staff to the Canadian Corps.

When that Last Post echoed away into the domed roof of the Menin Gate, the First World War seemed close enough to touch. There were veterans aplenty, although they were not always easy men to talk to. For some the war was, as the French survivor Jacques Meyer put it, 'our buried, secret youth', comprehensible, by definition, only to those who had shared the experience. Even if they did talk, Meyer argued that some troops built a linguistic wall of slang between themselves and outsiders. Others had become professional raconteurs, their fund of anecdotes worn smooth by frequent use. I learned to be cautious with both categories, though in different ways. The former might confide in you if they thought there was some point to it, so a little knowledge was essential, though it had to be very lightly worn. The latter might reveal something of merit, though only if they could be dissuaded from reminiscing about rats as big as footballs and the doubtful paternity of sergeant majors. The best were men who had never said much about the war but mused, as the years crept onwards, about their own demise, and wanted to say some things that they thought needed to be said. Nevertheless, one must always be cautious about the evidence of veterans: how might any of us remember and then describe a fatal car crash that happened forty years before?

As we approach the ninetieth anniversary of the war's end, I am conscious that the last Tommies, survivors of the biggest army this nation has ever put into the field, cannot live much longer. The last *poilu* went beyond recall by the thin trumpets of France while this book was in press. The war is about to pass beyond living memory and into history. In *Tommy* I began my story with words, letting the men who fought in the war speak for themselves, and using diaries, letters and other personal accounts when I could. Here I have started with pictures, and built my words around them. Despite my strictures against grabbing the usual suspects, there are some photographs which are simply too important not to use. Some are the pin-sharp work of official photographers. Others are the blurred product of amateurs' cameras. But it

Fig. 3

would be foolish not to include Fig. 3, taken by a member of the London Rifle Brigade, which shows his battalion's first waves attacking into the smoke and gas on the first day of the battle of Loos, 25 September 1915, or Fig. 4, Lieutenant C.A.F. Drummond's snapshot of soldiers of the Royal Warwickshire Regiment fraternising with Saxons of the 134th Infantry Regiment on Christmas Day 1914. However, I have tried to broaden my search, using photographs from regimental museums and private collections to supplement official images. For instance, the Liddle Collection's catalogue lists 782 sets of First World War photographs, yet few of them ever find their way into books. I have organised my chapters thematically rather than chronologically, and the images within them illustrate relevant aspects across all theatres in which British soldiers were engaged, though the majority are unsurprisingly of the Western Front.

Fig. 4

I

A Concourse of Men

The First World War was the largest event of world history until a greater catastrophe only a generation later. For Britain, though, it was not eclipsed even by the latter conflict. Almost twice as many British men and women served in the army in the First World War as did in the Second, and its human cost was unequalled in the nation's history. Britain and her Empire lost a million dead. That evasive term 'casualties' included not only killed, wounded and missing, but also soldiers interned in neutral countries. 1 July 1916, the first day of the Somme, remains Britain's bloodiest, just as the Somme itself, with its 420,000 British casualties, is the most costly battle the nation has ever fought. Perhaps its most iconic image is Fig. 5, which shows 103rd (Tyneside

Fig. 5

Irish) Brigade of 34th Division advancing on the Albert–Bapaume road, in the very centre of the first day's battle: the brigade lost over 2,000 casualties that day, and the division as a whole 6,300.

This shocking loss was brought about in part by the fact that this was the only war in modern history in which the British Army confronted the main force of a first-rate opponent in the conflict's principal theatre. During the French Revolutionary and Napoleonic Wars Britain furnished storm-tossed ships which helped throttle France, but generally contributed her land power only to secondary theatres like the Iberian Peninsula, and was virtually unrepresented in the great clashes of 1812–14 which wore down French military strength in central Europe. Indeed, the historian and strategist Basil Liddell Hart, whose perennial captaincy reflected his own ill-starred First World War service (he spent about six weeks at the front, and had no experience of the full flowering of the army's tactics in the war's last year), *Fig. 6* blamed the catastrophe of 1914–18 on the abandonment of what he called 'the

British way in warfare'. It was the Continental commitment, he maintained, the absurd determination to trade punch for punch with a heavyweight, rather than to ransack his dressing room, which accounted for the events which blighted his generation and seared themselves on his country's history.

A historian taking a longer view might argue that Allied victory in both world wars ultimately depended on the defeat of the German army in the field. In the First World War this was primarily accomplished on the Western Front by the French, the British and latterly the Americans. In the Second World War it was primarily achieved (though with crucial contributions to the erosion of German military and economic strength elsewhere) on the Eastern Front by the Russians.

The First World War left an enduring scar, made all the more livid because most of us encounter it as literature long before we confront its history. It is hard, having read Wilfred Owen's devastating condemnation of 'the old Lie: *Dulce et decorum est/Pro Patria mori*', not to be haunted by visions of men floundering in the mud, dropping in swathes to machine-gun fire, coughing up their lungs to gas, or twitching uncontrollably as they endlessly revisit a private hell. And it is not difficult, in a book concerned with the war's images, to find shots that confirm the very worst of our assumptions. Fig. 6 shows that abomination of desolation, the 1917 battlefield of Passchendaele, with a wrecked tank amongst water-filled shell-holes and ground exuding un-speakable foulness. Even more harrowing is Fig. 7, a body tossed into a tree by a shellburst. This was once a son, brother, husband or father. The demands imposed

Fig. 7

Fig. 8 on British manpower can be deduced from Fig. 8, eighteen-year-old conscripts photographed at the base camp of Étaples in the spring of 1918, too pathetically small for even the smallest size of army-issue trousers, destined for the front at a time that it was gulping infantrymen like a great carnivorous beast.

In Fig. 9 we can glimpse the destination of so much of this young flesh. Windmill Military Cemetery at Monchy le Preux, just east of Arras in northern France, was begun when the village was taken in April 1917, and some of the graves to the right rear date from this period. It was used until the ground was lost in the German offensive of March 1918, and was then used again from August to October that year as the British swept eastwards in the victorious advance of the Hundred Days. This photograph dates from the summer of 1918. Many of the bodies awaiting burial have all too evidently been killed by shellfire. Some have had their boots removed: the toes of one poor corpse are poking through his socks. Waterproof gas-capes give a shred of dignity, but one bloodied face, in the very centre of the photograph, tells us much about mortality.

Yet, while it would be absurd to set aside the poets' distillation of what Owen called 'the pity of War', it is dangerous to attribute a universality to the work of men like Owen, Siegfried Sassoon or Charles Sorley. One of the many virtues of Vivien Noakes's *Voices of Silence: The Alternative Book of First World War Poetry* (2006) was that it unveiled a wide variety of poems (some high-quality and others emphatically not) which give a broader view of the war than we might expect. There is humour, often rather dark, sentimentality, especially where mates and animals are concerned, and against all the odds, an adamantine thread of pride and even patriotism.

A.P. Herbert served in the 'Poor Bloody Infantry' in France and at Gallipoli, and was severely wounded, but wrote with deep affection of 'the lads who can live and can die/Backbone of the Empire, the old P.B.I.'. John Streets, a sergeant

Fig. 9

in the Sheffield Pals, was killed on the Somme in 1916. He wrote of seeing his comrades at dawn stand-to, when 'Men from the city, hamlet, town/Once white faces tanned to brown/Stand to the watch of the parapet/ . . . With a strange, proud look on every face/The SCORN of death, the PRIDE of race.' We should not assume that Streets, a Derbyshire miner, was necessarily more representative than the middle-class Owen: but we should neither rate the validity of men's judgements by the quality of their verse, nor think that, even for the infantry, the war was an unremittingly dismal experience.

What is true of poetry is no less valid for prose. I would include Siegfried Sassoon's trilogy – *Memoirs of a Foxhunting Man*, *Memoirs of an Infantry Officer* and *Sherston's Progress* – in my favourite dozen books about war. The fact of the matter, though, is that they were written in the 1930s, when they were very much 'emotion recollected in tranquillity'. Captain James Churchill Dunn, the medical officer of 2/Royal Welch Fusiliers, the battalion in which Sassoon served, had won the Distinguished Conduct Medal (second to the VC) in the South African War, and added both the Distinguished Service Order and Military Cross and Bar to it in 1914–18. He did not see the war in the same way as Sassoon and Robert Graves, another literary officer in the same battalion. Indeed, he fell out with the 'arrogantly wrong-headed' Graves, but remained on good terms with Sassoon. Dunn edited the battalion's unofficial history, *The War the Infantry Knew*, still one of the best books about the British Army on the Western Front. He was irritated by

> the catchpenny nature of so much of contemporary output [about the war] & the one sidedness of nearly all – the lurid side that gives a delicious shudder . . . I don't want the moods of the officers & men of the front line dished up second hand in the manner of Philip Gibbs and Beach Thomas: not distorted by facts and notions acquired after the war . . . nor ridiculed and caricatured by savage disillusion & revolt: nor mellowed to a form of art.

There is no question, though, of Dunn's war being sanitised. He described how in January 1916 an officer returning from leave met his company stretcher-bearers carrying a dead soldier down a communication trench.

Behind the stretcher-bearers came a man with a sandbag. 'Dewhurst asked "are those his effects?" ', for the personal possessions of the dead were sent home. He was told, 'No, sir, it's his pal': only fragments of a second victim of the same shell could be found. Yet on 1 March the same year St David's Day was celebrated with gusto. The quartermaster had organised a leek for everyone's cap, and the drummers had gilded the officers' leeks. 'No coherent account of that night was obtainable,' wrote Dunn, 'but there was evidence that one celebrant reached his billet, a quarter-mile distant, on all fours.' That June another officer described 'the beauty and tranquillity of the midsummer night. The sky was flawless but for a deep flounce of fleecy, dove-coloured cloud. Edged with bronze, all on the horizon ahead . . . I marched with young Crosland and his platoon most of the way . . . Poor boy! Three hours later he was dead.' And so it goes on: horror salved by humour, heroism softened by humility, and despair buttressed by duty, but with none of the easy clichés that are so often associated with the war.

Dunn's objection to the way that the war was being treated in contemporary prose (his book was first published in 1938) was echoed by other veterans. Charles Carrington, an infantry officer who won an MC at Passchendaele, lamented that 'dirt about the war was in demand. Every battle a defeat, every officer a nincompoop, every soldier a coward.' Part of the difficulty was the way in which popular attitudes to the war changed in the 1920s and 1930s. In great measure this was a consequence of the failure of returning veterans to find what David Lloyd George, Prime Minister for the last two years of the war, had called 'a fit country for heroes to live in'. For far too many of them the sense of comradeship and shared endeavour that emerges from accounts written during or soon after the war was swamped by the Depression. Looking through its grubby lenses, they came to see the conflict as a gigantic boss-class conspiracy which had betrayed their courage and wasted their comrades' sacrifice. Not all agreed. Alfred Pollard, a pre-war clerk who went to France as a sergeant in the Honourable Artillery Company in 1914 and was commissioned in 1916, won the VC, DCM and MC and Bar. The big, aggressive Pollard loved the war, and his book *Fire Eater* is arguably the closest any British author came to the German Ernst Jünger's celebration of combat in *Storm of Steel* (1920).

The war's images emphasise the danger of focusing exclusively on its dark side. Fig. 10 shows a party of officers and men of the 1/8th the King's Liverpool (The Liverpool Irish) after their return from a raid near Wailly on the night of 17–18 April 1916. Most are wearing cap-comforters, and a couple have added captured German spiked helmets to improve the shining hour. In Fig. 11 a company of Royal Fusiliers have just returned from a successful operation in 1918, and once again joy is unconfined: these are not men constrained by fear of the officer's pistol or the firing squad. The company commander, squarely in the centre, is exuberant. He has swapped his Sam Browne for a soldier's belt and webbing pistol holster but, despite GHQ's unequivocal order that officers taking part in assaults were to dress in the same way as the men they led, he is still wearing his rank-stars on his cuffs, although his brother officers have wisely shifted theirs to their shoulders. Something of the sense of comradeship that helped get men through can be seen in Fig. 12. These three men have just come out of the line: two wear trench waders over their boots and puttees, and all are cold and filthy. The

Fig. 10 (opposite top)

Fig. 11 (opposite bottom)

Fig. 12

original caption tells us that the photographer is an officer, but it is clear from his mates' expressions that the centre soldier, shovelling a huge spoonful of mashed potato into his mouth, is engaged in a wind-up.

There were hard times after the war as well as during it. Even Pollard, unquestionably a war hero and latterly a prolific author, for a time found it hard to make ends meet, and even tried to pawn his decorations. The majority of returning soldiers fared much worse. Few of them would deny that the war had given them a sense of comradeship which exceeded anything they encountered before or since in their civilian lives. Charles Douie, who had earned an MC with the Dorsets, thought that 'the men who had never lost hope in the darkest hours of 1918' now faced unemployment 'without the support of either the old comradeship or the old faith'.

With the change in attitude to the war came the need to find someone to blame for it, and there was growing criticism of generals and their staff, with Field Marshal Douglas Haig, British commander-in-chief on the Western Front from late 1915 till the end of the war, becoming the villain of the piece. He died in 1928, having devoted the latter years of his life to the British Legion, founded in 1921 from four organisations which had tried to safeguard the interests of those who had fought. Partly because of this evident commitment to the men he had served with, criticism was muted during his lifetime, but Winston Churchill's *The World Crisis* (1923) and then David Lloyd George's *War Memoirs* (1933–36) attacked both the primacy of the Western Front and the conduct of operations there. Lloyd George, as the man in overall charge of British policy in the year of Passchendaele, had sound personal reasons for offloading responsibility for a battle which had come to epitomise all that was terrible about the war and sterile in Britain's approach to it.

The tendency to see the war in terms of lions led by donkeys accelerated markedly in the 1960s, with Alan Clark's *The Donkeys* (1961) the most striking example of a genre in which authors told their readers all the dismal things they yearned to hear. Clark's book had a great influence on Joan Littlewood's musical *Oh! What a Lovely War* (1963), which was turned into a film in 1969. During the 1960s some historians had begun to use the documents then made available to them by the reduction of the closure period for public records from fifty to thirty years, but the process of reappraisal has proved long and painful, and even now, at the ninetieth anniversary of the end of the war, the popular cursor tends to flick back remorselessly to those images sketched out in the 1920s, that sepia landscape splashed with woeful crimson.

In *Tommy* (2004) I used a wealth of material written during the war to suggest that, whatever veterans might have thought in the 1930s, during and immediately after the fighting the British soldier might best be summed up by the single word 'enduring'. This was not an army teetering on the edge of mutiny. For all that has been written about capital courts-martial (a process which, let it be said, fills me with horror), it is evident that most of those executed were lawfully condemned by the law as it then stood. The granting of posthumous pardons in 2007 tells us far more about ourselves than it does about my grandfathers' generation. The historian Victor Davis Hanson warns us that modern affluent societies take a therapeutic and managerial view of human experience rather than the tragic view taken by our ancestors. He goes on to suggest that this shapes our approach to modern conflict, which we expect 'to be waged in accordance with warranties, law suits and product recalls, and adjudicated by judges and lawyers in stale courtrooms rather than won or lost by often emotional youth in the filth, confusion and barbarity of the battlefield'.

It is important neither to view the war through the prism of the present, nor to fiddle with it to make it fit any particular conceptual framework. The experience of individual soldiers ran the full spectrum. At one extreme there were those like J.B. Priestley, who had volunteered as a private, become a 'temporary gentleman', and who saw the whole business as a deadly waste of time: 'the giant locusts . . . had eaten my four and a half years'. At the other, the much-decorated Adrian Carton de Wiart declared: 'Frankly I had enjoyed the war; it had given me many bad moments, lots of good ones, plenty of excitement and with everything found for us.'

Any unit contained a variable proportion of thrivers, survivors and skivers. In the same little communal cemetery at Ors, not far from Landrecies in northern France, with the graves of fifty-nine men all killed in the last weeks of the war, lie both the poet Lieutenant Wilfred Owen MC of the Manchesters and Lieutenant Colonel James Neville Marshall of the Irish Guards, killed

Fig. 13

commanding 16/Lancashire Fusiliers on 4 November 1918. Fig. 13 shows Marshall with a fine row of decorations – he had served in the Belgian army at the start of the war, earning the Order of Leopold and the Croix de Guerre. There are already eight wound-stripes on his cuff, and the rosette denoting a second award has not yet been added to his purple-and-white Military Cross ribbon. Yet the fact that he had already felt war's sharp edge did not persuade him to hang back. On the day he died, 'a partly constructed bridge' over the Sambre–Oise canal

was broken before the advanced troops of his battalion could cross. Lt Col Marshall at once went forward and organised parties to repair the bridge. The first party were soon killed or wounded, but by personal example he inspired his command, and volunteers were instantly forthcoming. Under intense fire and with complete disregard of his own safety, he stood on the bank encouraging his men and assisting in the work, and when the bridge was repaired attempted to rush across at the head of his battalion and was killed while doing so.

This quotation comes from his VC citation.

For many, willy-nilly, there was an absorption into the army's communal life. David Jones, the author of *In Parenthesis*, described his battalion of the Royal Welch Fusiliers on the march.

> Some like tight belts and some like loose belts – trussed up pockets – cigarettes in ammunition pouches – rifle-bolts, webbing, buckles and rain – gotta light mate – give us a match chum. How cold the morning is and blue, and how mysterious in cupped hands glow the match-lights of a concourse of men, moving so early in the morning.

Fig. 14 (*overleaf*), showing troops marching up the Albert–Amiens road in November 1916, has little to recommend it as a photograph. We might perhaps crop those last few figures to grab a moustachioed face glancing emptily back at the photographer, but although the curved cloth shoulder-titles tell us that this is a Guards battalion, there is little sense of time or place. This is precisely its charm. It is a battalion, any battalion, marching by companies, at ease in column of fours, somewhere in France. Company commanders have wisely dismounted to share the road with their men: a spurred heel is just visible on the last foot on the photograph's right. Cookers, already heating up the next meal, follow each company, like smoky markers at the end of its line of march. There is probably a song on the go, not soul-stirring or patriotic, but as irreverent and endless as the road ahead.

> *We don't want ham*
> *lamb or jam – we don't want*
> *roly-po—ly . . .*

For some who remembered incompetent officers and bullying NCOs, there were others, like Adolphus ('Dolph') Jupe of 1/9th Hampshires, who reflected:

> I suppose in our lives we give our hearts unrestrainedly to very few things. I had given mine to the Battalion and bore its three stripes upon my arms with greater pride than I have ever experienced since. We had worn a proud uniform for over

Fig. 14
(overleaf)

five years and with many others I was disconsolate at its putting off. For the sufferings, the sacrifice and the heroism of a million men of our generation whose bones lay at rest across the sea, had raised the prestige of our race to a height never before achieved, and even upon us, however faintly, was reflected the glory of their achievements.

And of course there were others who never had the chance to look back, be it with pride, anguish or fury, on their service, for they were killed before they had left any mark on the war. Let two speak for many. John Hopkinson, in Fig. 15, the son of Walter and Alice Hopkinson of Butts Road, Ashover, joined the army at Chesterfield on 11 February 1915. He was thirty years and eight months old at the time, and gave his occupation as boot repairer. Married to Annie, an Ashover girl, he had two children, Edwin, born on 5 August 1909, and Wilfred, born on 23 September 1914, and three brothers, Frank, Harry and Wilfred. John Hopkinson was photographed during his brief military career. Although shaving the upper lip was at that time forbidden by army regulations, like many new recruits John remained clean-shaven, and so there is little to give him a martial aspect. Perhaps that dandyism which encouraged recruits to look their best in their first portrait in uniform has inspired him to get hold of collar badges bearing the regimental Bengal tiger topped by a rose, irreverently known as 'the cat and cabbage'. These 'collar dogs' were rarely worn on active service except by officers.

John was posted to France on 1 May 1915, and was sent to 1/York and Lancaster, then fighting for its life on Frezenberg Ridge, just north of Ypres. On 8 May the Germans, pressing the advantage they had gained by their use of gas in late April, launched an attack backed by overwhelming artillery. After five days' fighting they had gained perhaps 1,000 yards: not all unconstructive attacks were British. In the process they killed John Hopkinson, on the first day of their attack, on his first day in action, and probably on his first day with the battalion. We can only guess what use he would have been with just six weeks' training, all the time it

Fig. 15

Fig. 16

took to process him from boot repairer to corpse. He has no known grave, and is commemorated, as we see in Fig. 16, on the Menin Gate at Ypres.

While he was away his wife had received a separation allowance of 17s.6d. a week, and he made an 'allotment of pay' to her of another 5s.3d. a week. From 17 January 1916 she was awarded a pension of 18s.6d. a week for herself and her two sons. When told that her husband was missing, Annie Hopkinson hoped (as so many did) that he might have been taken prisoner or picked up wounded, and after the war she advertised for news of him in the *Derbyshire Times* (Fig. 17), though with no result.

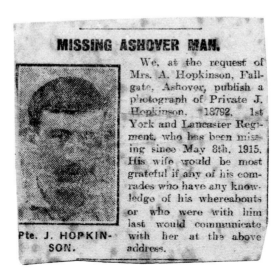

Fig. 17

John's brother Wilfred Hopkinson enlisted in the 9/York and Lancaster, a New Army battalion which formed at Pontefract in 1914. One of the four battalions in 70th Brigade, part of the 23rd Division, it went to France in August 1915, but the brigade was almost immediately transferred to the regular 8th Division, one of whose brigades was moved across to 'stiffen' the 23rd. On 1 July 1916 the 8th Division attacked, its three brigades side by side, just north of the main Albert to Bapaume road which bisects the Somme battlefield. The leading two battalions of 70th Brigade, on its left, got into the German front trenches, though at heavy cost. As the *Official History* records, 9/York and Lancaster, ordered forward to support them, found that:

> The machine-gun fire from the Thiepval spur, which enfiladed the advance at a range of six hundred to eight hundred yards, now greatly increased. The battalion lost fifty percent of its men almost at once, and very few men reached the German front trench.

When 11/Sherwood Foresters in turn tried to follow up, they had to 'literally step over the corpses of the York & Lancaster which had preceded them'. The brigade was the hardest-hit in the division, with just under 2,000 casualties, including all four of its commanding officers. Wilfred Hopkinson was killed and, like his brother John, has no known grave, but is commemorated on the Thiepval Memorial (Fig. 18).

Fig. 18

Fig. 19

Wilfred, in Fig. 19, has cultivated a formidable moustache, and wears his brass regimental shoulder titles but no collar-dogs. He has a leather bandolier from the 1903 pattern equipment. Bandoliers designed for mounted troops had nine pouches, five at the front and four at the back, holding ninety rounds of .303 rifle ammunition, while the infantry version had only five pouches. The fact that Wilfred is wearing the waist-belt from the 1908 webbing equipment testifies to the fact that there were often too few sets of homogeneous equipment to go round. Company sergeant majors hated seeing their men in a mixture of leather and webbing equipment, and usually tried to standardise on webbing if they could. Private Will Wells of the Manchester Regiment recalled that when his battalion arrived in France in early 1916, 'We were told to hand in our old leather equipment and were given salvaged sets of webbing. Mine was stiff with dried blood, and I swapped it for a decent set as soon as I could.'

In one important sense the First World War owes its enduring grasp on our folk memory to the fact that it was the first real photographer's war. Louis Daguerre and an associate developed a commercial photographic process in the 1830s. Roger Fenton took photographs of the Crimean War, Felice Beato photographed the Indian Mutiny, and Matthew Brady and

Alexander Gardner caught aspects of the American Civil War in a striking series of shots that brought the casual squalor of bodies strewn about a desolate landscape to a mass audience for the first time, for photography, unlike painting, allowed images of war to be mass-produced. Brady, reported the *New York Times*, 'has done something to bring home to us the terrible reality and earnestness of war'.

The technical limitations of early photography meant that its practitioners could photograph only stationary or posed scenes, which is one of the reasons the dead, with their swollen bodies, bulging tunics and burst buttons, were such an attractive target. Photographers could freeze uncertain young men in their martial glory, catch carefully-grouped soldiers, or find the jetsam of battle once its tide had boiled past. 'Action shots' were beyond them, and they were sometimes not above rearranging the dead, like props on their set, to make for better pictures. The camera often lied, then as now.

By the First World War all this had changed. The first Kodak camera had appeared in 1888, and the first Brownie in 1900: the latter's rollfilm, spooled on between shots and then sent off for development, made possible the snapshot as we know it. One officer helpfully annotated his photographs, now in the Liddle Collection in the Brotherton Library at the University of Leeds, 'Taken with my 2A Brownie.' Alongside small, easily portable cameras like this were larger plate cameras, generally more cumbersome and less forgiving, but capable of taking fine high-definition stills. Moving film, too, was just beginning to make its presence felt, with the first 35mm cine camera appearing in 1914.

Many officers, and rather fewer soldiers, took cameras to war with them in 1914, and, despite official disapproval, snapped away when the opportunity offered. For example, Lieutenant Robert Cotton Money went to war as machine-gun officer of 1/Cameronians in August 1914. He claimed that he had never heard of any order banning cameras, carried one on his belt, and sent dozens of photographs back to Glasgow to be developed. Some of these found their way into the newspapers, where they were accredited to 'an officer serving at the front'. Money distributed his photographs widely amongst his brother officers, and there are collections in both the Imperial War Museum's photographic archive and the Liddle Archive. Lieutenant Colonel Thomas

Tait Pitman, commanding the 11th Hussars at the beginning of the war and a cavalry division at its end, took numerous photographs of the cavalry in 1914–15. Some percolated their way through to the Imperial War Museum, but the original albums are in the regimental museum of the King's Royal Hussars in Winchester. In the summer of 1915 G.M. Liddle, then a private in the Honourable Artillery Company, told his parents: 'Am sending back a camera film by a man going on leave. Anyone found with one after today is to be put under arrest.' However, what was risky for a private was far safer for an officer, and, duly commissioned into the Royal Field Artillery (he finished the war a captain with a Military Cross), Liddle took many more photographs. Cost was a constraint for some: Sergeant R. Harrison of the Royal Warwicks, a Gallipoli veteran, paid 1s.4d. (half a day's pay) to have a spool of film developed.

Then there were the accidental soldiers. In 1914 Paul Maze, son of a well-to-do Le Havre merchant, was so charmed by seeing British cavalry in bivouac on their way to the front that he got himself attached to the Royal Scots Greys as interpreter. Maze was already well on the way to being an artist in his own right, and ended his days in Sussex in 1979, sometimes described as 'the last impressionist'. He became a well-respected figure, earning the Distinguished Conduct Medal and Military Medal as well as the friendship of Winston Churchill, and his ambivalent status helped him take photographs where a camera in other hands might not have been welcome.

Another unofficial photographer was Frederic Abernethy Coleman, an American citizen who was one of the twenty members of the Royal Automobile Club who put themselves and their cars at the army's disposal in 1914. Stout, jolly (despite the loss of his car to shell-fire) and well-connected, Coleman wore an officer's uniform with no badges of rank, and eventually published *From Mons to Ypres with French* and *With the Cavalry on the Western Front*. It is easy to miss his work, but an album in the King's Royal Hussars museum contains a picture of him looking rather like a jovially unkempt bear, with the marginal annotation: 'Frederic Coleman, who took all the pictures (this size).'

Even in 1914 there were many other amateur photographers: most regimental museums are full of their work, often uncatalogued and unidentified, and frequently, as one might expect, showing the familiar features of Alf, Bert and Percy (or indeed Vandeleur, O'Callaghan and Tyndale-Biscoe) against a

Fig. 20
(previous
pages)

shell-ploughed landscape or on the cobbles of a Flanders town, intensely interesting to their descendants but of narrower merit for the historian. Before long their professional colleagues from the press were also busy, though subject to practical constraints – getting access to the front line was rarely a simple matter, which tended to make them better at recording scenes behind the lines than they were at catching the face of battle. French commercial photographers joined in, and companies like Stévenard in Dunkirk and Lelong in Amiens produced postcards, typically showing war-damaged towns or uncontroversially cheery soldiers. There were a few civilian photographers whose work is all the more telling for being wholly unstaged. Fig. 20 (*previous pages*), taken by a Belgian civilian, shows A Company 4/Royal Fusiliers in the Grande Place of the little Belgian town of Mons on 22 August 1914, the day before the battalion made its name by defending the Mons–Condé canal, winning the first VCs of the war.

It was not until March 1916 that the British, responding to a public appetite whetted by striking but unofficial photographs of the fighting at

Fig. 21

Gallipoli, appointed their first official photographer. Ernest Brooks, who had worked for the pictorial newspaper the *Daily Mirror* and been at Gallipoli, was a natural choice. Brooks and his colleagues – there were eventually perhaps a dozen in all – were commissioned as lieutenants, wore uniform, were subject to military discipline, and their work was censored. However, this control affected the release of their images for publication rather than their decisions over what to photograph. As we will see, there was no prohibition against photographing British dead, although the authorities were anxious to ensure that their faces or those of the badly wounded were not recognisable. Fig. 21 is Brooks' work, and shows a British soldier in a trench at Guillemont on the Somme, probably killed by the same shellburst that has scattered chalk and earth over his body as if prefiguring the act of burial. Brooks took about 4,400 photographs of the Western Front, roughly a fifth of the British official total.

Even a professional photographer's judgement might fail him. Fig. 22 shows an army carpenter planing a cross for a comrade's grave. His improvised

Fig. 22

workbench has the chalked designation 'C Sub', for C Subsection (the gun and wagon which formed a sergeant's command), so we can guess that he is a member of the Royal Artillery. On the right, however, is that rarely photographed structure, an officers' latrine, and the carpenter seems to be using its urinal section in which to store his off-cuts.

Oddly enough, there were official movie cameramen at work in France before the first official stills photographer arrived. In November 1915 Geoffrey Malins and Edward Tong, both newly-commissioned lieutenants, began work. Tong was soon invalided home, but Malins had made twenty-six films by the summer of 1916. The authorities decided, controversially, to allow him and his new colleague, John McDowell, to film the year's major offensive, and it was estimated that *The Battle of the Somme* was seen by some twenty million people – almost half the population of the United Kingdom. We now know that many shots apparently showing the attack on the morning of 1 July had in fact been taken earlier, and a number of explosions were filmed not on the chalk uplands north of Albert, but at the army's trench-mortar training school. However, among the authentic clips was a sequence showing the explosion of the mine beneath Hawthorn Ridge Redoubt, just west of Beaumont Hamel, which has become the standard archive clip used by documentary producers who wish to illustrate any First World War mine. Malins was probably never a comfortable man, and his wartime experience did not make him any easier: he was gassed, wounded several times, and eventually invalided out of the army. His 1920 book *How I Filmed the War* is an immodest account of his achievements, although he deserves recognition for producing the first film to show a battle while it was still in progress. Fig. 23 shows Malins (right, in a Burberry trenchcoat) standing beside Ernest Brooks at a tea stall in the rear of the Somme battlefield in 1916.

The combination of unofficial and official photographs, as well as single frames captured from Malins' work, provides an extraordinarily rich source of evidence. However, just as the most telling personal accounts of the war tend to get overused, so historians illustrating their work on the war often collar the usual suspects. The shot of soldiers with helmet, rifle and pack trudging in single file in front of a turbulent skyline is a hardy perennial, occasionally used with the image reversed (whether from sheer carelessness or to

break the thread of familiarity it is hard to say), just as the distant shot of *Fig. 23* stretcher-bearer in a crater-field-blighted landscape is sometimes cropped to emphasise the figures and diminish the landscape. Sometimes this happens because authors brief their picture researchers on the basis of what they themselves have seen in other books, and so the same images get used and re-used. And, just as we must apply healthy scepticism to written accounts (Who is telling us this? How did he know? And when did he write it down?), so too we must be cautious about photographic evidence.

Mistrust any photograph taken from in front of a weapon's muzzle: this was never a healthy place to be if the weapon was loaded or there was any serious prospect of incoming fire. Riflemen intending to shoot had their forefinger on the trigger, and Vickers machine-gunners were unable to traverse along the enemy's parapet unless they had first put a belt of ammunition into their weapon. Field telephones worked better when connected to a cable, and artillery genuinely in action, not filmed at gun-drill behind the lines, tended to be surrounded by live shells, neatly stacked, and empty cases, chucked down anyhow.

Captions in archives are sometimes wrong, and an error, once made, is likely to be repeated *ad infinitum*. For instance, a sequence of photographs of British troops just behind the September 1915 battlefield of Loos (one of which appears in Fig. 24) was, for many years, blithely captioned to August 1914. Very often the devil is in the detail. The floppy 'gorblimey' cap – officially Winter Service Dress, but allegedly earning its name from the exasperation of the first sergeant major to set his affronted eyes on it – appeared in late 1914, and was rarely seen after the summer of 1916. The distinctive ribbon of the Military Cross – like the fat-barrelled Lewis gun – appeared in early 1915, and the steel helmet ('tin hat') first appeared in the British Army in the spring of 1916: Dr Dunn got his on 9 March. Units are often wrongly captioned, though non-commissioned personnel wore brass shoulder titles on each epaulette bearing either their unit's name, as in 'Queens' for the Queen's Royal West Surrey Regiment, or its initials, as in 'RFA' for Royal Field Artillery, and many photographs are sharp enough for these to be identified.

On 1 August 1917, when British strength on the Western Front peaked, there were 1,721,000 British, 147,000 Australian and New Zealand, 144,000 Canadian, and 8,000 South African soldiers there, as well as 24,000 Indian Army troops (British and Indian), and 90,000 non-combatant native troops, most of them labourers – a grand total of well over two million officers and men. At the height of the Dardanelles campaign in 1915 there were some 80,000 British and Dominion forces at Gallipoli, as well as a French contingent whose presence is too often overlooked. British and Dominion troops at Salonika, whose lack of strategic impact encouraged the Germans to quip that the place was a huge internment camp, peaked at around 250,000 in mid-1917, and in the spring of 1918 there were 182,000 officers and men in northern Italy. For the whole of the last year of the war there were around a quarter of a million men fighting the Turks in Mesopotamia (modern Iraq). Although the war in Africa was on a much smaller scale than that in other theatres, British combatant strength in East Africa and Uganda peaked at 58,000 in September 1917. Rather under half the soldiers who fought there were actually in the British Army, and the combatant element

Fig. 24

– British, Indian and South African – was supported by a native labour force of around 140,000.

No study of the British Army can neglect the contribution made by the Empire and the Dominions, nor should it ignore the corollary, that the war helped to forge Australian and Canadian national identities. The issue has too often become politicised, not least in arguments about the relative fighting quality of national contingents. Suffice it to say that the Allies could not have won the war without Britain's contribution, which depended, in its turn, upon the assistance given, for instance, by Australians at Gallipoli or Pozières, Canadians at Second Ypres and Vimy, New Zealanders on the Somme or at Passchendaele, and South Africans at Delville Wood. In selecting photographs I have concentrated on those of British soldiers, for they are my subject, but there will be times when we see Australians filling jam-tin bombs at Gallipoli, steel-helmeted Canadian cavalry going forward at Cambrai, or sepoys carrying a wounded sahib on a stretcher.

Although there are some big landscapes and open beaches, my concern is with people rather than places, for this is a book about the soldier and his experience, not a history of the war or a discourse on its strategy. My subject was aged somewhere between fourteen and sixty-eight, and served from the *beeks* of Flanders to the chalklands of Champagne, from the foothills of the Dolomites to the islands of the Aegean, and from the Pyramids to the great gates of Babylon. He was part of the widest possible social cross-section. On the one hand, so great was the damage done to the peerage and baronetage in the first six months of the war that no edition of *Debrett's* was published in the spring of 1915, as its editors had been unable to bring the work up to date: not since the Wars of the Roses had so many aristocrats met violent deaths. Lady Elizabeth Bowes-Lyon, later Queen Elizabeth the Queen Mother, had a brother, Captain the Hon. Fergus Bowes-Lyon of the Black Watch, killed at Loos in 1915; one cousin, Lieutenant Charles Lindsay Claude Bowes-Lyon, killed at Ypres in October 1914; and another, Lieutenant Gavin Patrick Bowes-Lyon, killed at Cambrai in 1917. On the other hand, 1,000 men from Lord Leverhulme's works at Port Sunlight volunteered at once to form 11/Cheshire, and without miners, with their own proud and edgy sense of tribal identity, it is hard to see how the war could have been fought at all. One of its finest VCs was won by a middle-aged miner from Manvers Main colliery in South Yorkshire, who stood by his mate in the face of certain death from sliding earth (see page 162).

Some were heroes. In the history of the Victoria Cross only three men have earned a second award. One, Arthur Martin-Leake, won his Cross in the Boer War and a Bar to it in the First World War, and another, Noel Chavasse, won both Cross and Bar (and an MC into the bargain) on the Western Front. Some were villains: fifteen British soldiers (including one officer) were executed for murder, often because they settled an old score (or imagined a new one) when in drink. Some looked the part, polished their buttons and tied their puttees neatly. Others were the bane of sergeant majors and an embarrassment to their mates. They are all here, those 'legions who have suffered and are dust', this great concourse of men, frozen for ever by the photographers who made this war their own.

2

Flesh and Blood

We cannot understand the British Army of the First World War without grasping an essential truth. The conflict saw a tiny peacetime army swell into the biggest force Britain has ever put into the field, a process which would have proved taxing even if it had not been accompanied by the need to fight a bitter war, at a time of marked technological change, against an accomplished enemy. In 1914 Britain had 247,423 regular officers and men, backed by an army reserve of ex-regulars 145,347 strong, as well as 63,933 members of the Special Reserve, who had carried out six months' training, kept topped up by another two weeks a year. The Territorial Force, not liable for service overseas unless individuals voluntarily undertook to accept an 'Imperial Service' obligation, had 268,777 officers and men. All in all, Britain had 733,514 regulars and reservists at her disposal when the war began. Germany, in contrast, had a peacetime standing army of 700,000 men, inflated by mobilisation to 3.7 million.

While the German army was trained and equipped for continental war on a massive scale, no British soldier had fired a shot in western Europe since the last round thudded out on the battlefield of Waterloo ninety-nine years before. Britain's military experience had been largely colonial. However, 'staff conversations' with the French, which began in 1906, produced a plan to send an Expeditionary Force of around 100,000 men to France in the event of a German attack. This was a significant departure from previous British policy, and would require political approval before it could be implemented. The BEF was to take position around Maubeuge, on the very left of the French line. This would give the British an unconstricted line of communication from Le Havre, where most would land, through Amiens, to the concentration area. Perhaps more important, though, was the fact that the French believed (as confidently as wrongly) that the Germans would not come through Belgium, and that if political approval for the deployment of the BEF was not forthcoming the French plan, for a do-or-die offensive straight across the Franco–German border, would not be compromised by the absence of the British.

The regulars of 1914 were poor men officered by rather richer ones, though like most rules this one had exceptions. William Robertson, son of a Lincolnshire village tailor, came from the artisan class which traditionally looked down on service in the ranks, but he enlisted as a cavalry private in 1877, and was commissioned eleven years later at the age of twenty-eight. He went to France in 1914 as quartermaster general (principal logistic staff officer) of the BEF, became Chief of the Imperial General Staff in December 1915, and died a field marshal and a baronet. Slightly more typical were John Lucy and his brother Denis, middle-class boys who grew tired of life in a small southern Irish town after their mother died, and enlisted in the Royal Irish Rifles. John was later commissioned and became a lieutenant colonel in the Second World War. Denis was killed in action in 1914: John last saw him well ahead of his section, leading the boys straight.

For the overwhelming majority of regular NCOs and men, the army offered escape from unemployment or drudgery. Its infantry structure was intended to create firm links between regiments, their recruiting districts and the men who duly signed up. The system was much less successful in practice than it seems in proud retrospect. Between 1883 and 1900 only nineteen line infantry regiments drew more than half their men from their districts, thirty took between a quarter and half, and sixteen (including some of the most distinguished Highland Scots regiments) less than a quarter. However, once a man had joined, the regiment's traditions and tribal markings helped foster his sense of identity. So too did long evenings spent quaffing thin beer in the 'wet canteen' or heading into town, boots polished and buttons gleaming, for something more potable. Soldiers were not always easy men: Kipling had wisely observed that 'single men in barracks don't grown into plaster saints', and Frank Richards, perennial private in the Royal Welch Fusiliers, frankly admitted that 'booze and fillies' were the constant preoccupations of his comrades.

Most regiments had two regular battalions, usually one in the United Kingdom and the other abroad. The Bedfordshire Regiment traced its lineage back to the 16th Foot, raised in 1688. In 1914 its 1st Battalion was at Mullingar in southern Ireland, whence it mobilised as part of 15th Brigade of 5th Division, and its 2nd Battalion was in Pretoria, returning to England that September to form part of 7th Division. In Fig. 25 we see the drums of 1/Bedfords leading the battalion back down the Farnborough Road from the garrison church of All Saints in a church parade in Aldershot in 1913, shortly before the battalion left for Ireland. Its officers and men are wearing scarlet tunics with white facings: the dress regulations of 1902 had prescribed blue facings for royal and white for non-royal regiments, but some regiments soon reverted to facings of traditional hue, like the Hampshires' yellow and the grass green of the Dorsets. The 1881 pattern home service helmet, worn with a spike on top by the infantry and with a ball-top by artillery and engineers, was much influenced by the German *pickelhaube*, and testifies to the tendency for armies to ape the dress and equipment of the dominant force of the age. The army had bought its first

Fig. 25

49

Fig. 26   parcel of land at Aldershot in 1854, and by 1914 Aldershot Command was the army's biggest garrison, and most of its units mobilised to form I Corps of the BEF, under Lieutenant General Sir Douglas Haig.

Those who joined the army as regular officers very often came from military backgrounds: in 1910, 43.1 per cent of the gentleman cadets entering Sandhurst, which trained officers for the infantry, cavalry and supporting services, had fathers who were 'military professionals'. Most cadets had been to public schools, where many would have served in the Junior Division of the Officers' Training Corps, simply 'the corps' to generations of schoolboys, in which they could earn 'Certificate A', the first step on the road to a commission. Contingent sizes varied, with Eton providing a full battalion, Cheltenham four companies, and some smaller public and grammar schools a single company. The cadet company at Wolverhampton Grammar School (Fig. 26) wore a cap badge based on the arms of Sir Stephen Jenyns, who had founded the school in 1512.

Some 116 old boys of the school were to die in the war, most as officers or NCOs, and their obituaries in the school magazine chart the bleeding of a generation. Second Lieutenant Douglas William Armitage died at Loos in 1915: 'tired, cold and hungry, he was last seen fighting with his fists and since then no more has been heard of him'. George Murphy had left school to read medicine at Birmingham University, but joined up on the outbreak of war and was killed in the infantry at Passchendaele, where 'most of his gunners were put out of action [and] he was seen serving a Lewis gun himself until he was shot through the head. It is interesting to recall that Lieutenant Murphy acted as judge in the House Squad Competition in our OTC in 1915.' Fig. 26 probably shows the OTC members of a house, with their house master at the centre of the group. Some of the cadets are wearing officer-style breeches, and it is not hard to see some of them making an easy transition to adult service and, no doubt, the roll of honour too.

Eight universities had contingents of the Senior Division of the OTC, where a man could gain 'Certificate B', qualifying for a Territorial commission. R.B. Haldane, Secretary of State for War 1905–12, whose reforms were intended to remedy the deficiencies revealed in the Anglo–Boer war of 1899–1902, hoped that the OTCs would both officer the Territorial Force and strengthen the links between army and society. Cambridge University OTC, formed from Cambridge University Volunteer Rifle Corps, had a squadron of cavalry, a section of field artillery, a company of fortress engineers, a signals section, an infantry battalion and a field ambulance section. These OTC members, photographed some time before the war (Fig. 27, *overleaf*), are probably an infantry company, with their captain in the centre. To his right sits the company's colour sergeant, wearing the corps' full-dress uniform of 'French grey' with light-blue collar and cuffs. The corps, unusually, had a Boer War battle honour, earned by a student contingent who volunteered to join the Suffolk Regiment. Cambridgeshire had no regular regiment of its own, but was in the Suffolks' recruiting area.

The cost of being a regular officer varied from regiment to regiment. In 1903 a War Office committee thought that an officer needed at least £160 a year in addition to his pay, and in the cavalry, where an officer had to provide himself with at least one charger and would be expected to hunt and play polo, he might just scrape by with £300 a year, but most cavalry officers had twice as much at their disposal. One young officer who had been *Fig. 27 (overleaf)*

commissioned in the economical Royal Field Artillery and had only £18 a year to add to his annual pay of £74 found it exceptionally hard to make ends meet.

A substantial private income was essential for young men who hoped for commissions in the Brigade of Guards. There were then four regiments of foot guards, the Grenadier, the Coldstream, the Scots and the Irish, the latter formed in 1900 to reward Irish gallantry in South Africa. The Irish Guards' badge (cap star in guardee) was the star of the Order of St Patrick, and its tunic buttons were arranged in fours. The officers in Fig. 28, photographed in 1914, are wearing service dress, with the bronzed buttons generally worn by officers, and stylish forage hats, replaced on active service by khaki caps. Foot guards officers had badges of rank on their epaulettes rather than their cuffs, and all wear the Sam Browne belt, named for the one-armed General Sir Sam Browne, whose cross-strap (sometimes worn doubled, like braces) helped *Fig. 28* take the weight of sword and pistol. Service dress tunics were made of

Fig. 29

substantial material (dark khaki barathea for the foot guards, whipcord for many other regiments), and officers wore them with breeches, puttees and brown boots. Dress regulations prescribed dark khaki for both ties and breeches, but they were often sported in much lighter shades. One irritable brigadier general asked a colonel where on earth his adjutant got his (rather light) shirts from, only to be told that they doubtless came from the same shop as the general's aide de camp's breeches.

The officer with fashionably light breeches is Lieutenant the Hon. Harold Alexander, son of the Earl of Caledon, commissioned into the regiment in 1912. He was a much-decorated temporary brigadier general by the end of the war, and died as Field Marshal Sir Harold Alexander, 1st Earl Alexander of Tunis and Errigol in the County of Donegal. The Irish Guards fought on the Western Front from first to last, losing their commanding officer, Lieutenant Colonel the Hon. George Morris, in 1914. Rudyard Kipling's son Jack was killed with the regiment at Loos the following year, and Kipling wrote its fine history, *The Irish Guards in the Great War*. The burden which fell on pre-war regulars can be gauged from Fig. 29, a photograph of the officers of 1/Royal Fusiliers on mobilisation at Parkstone Barracks on the Isle of Wight on 14 August 1914. Of the thirty-one officers in the photograph, sixteen were to be killed and eleven wounded, mostly within the next six months. Lieutenant

Fig. 30

Maurice Dease (top row, second from left) was killed winning the Victoria Cross at the railway bridge at Nimy, just north of Mons, on 23 August 1914.

The cost of serving as an officer in a Territorial unit was high in the case of yeomanry (Territorial cavalry) regiments, whose officers might have to turn out furred and frogged in the splendour of hussar full dress (the serious-looking officer in Fig. 30 is Lieutenant and Bandmaster H.G. Amers of the Northumberland Hussars), but was more modest for Territorial battalions of county regiments. The smarter London Territorial units were part gentleman's sporting and social club, and part infantry battalion. The London Rifle Brigade, whose headquarters in Bunhill Row included a large drill hall which doubled as 'a first-class gym', had traditionally charged an entrance fee of one guinea, and expected an annual subscription of the same amount. When it became part of the new Territorial Force in 1908, taking the formal title 5th (City of London) Battalion the London Regiment, it continued to demand payment, in common with units like the Artists' Rifles and the London Scottish. Men joining after the outbreak of war in 1914 were charged their first quarter-year fee in advance, and in the spring of 1915 there were some complaints that subscription money was docked from pay, though this continued until the practice was banned by Parliament after the introduction of conscription a year later.

It is small wonder that when the young Allan Harding, a Post Office Savings Bank clerk, wanted a Territorial commission in May 1914 he applied, not to a unit that had stockbrokers serving happily in its ranks, but to 11th Battalion the London Regiment, the Finsbury Rifles. This was known, from the location of its headquarters in Penton Street and the alcoholic propensities of its members, as the Pentonville Pissers. He was an acting lieutenant colonel by the war's end, and died Field Marshal Lord Harding of Petherton, having in the process adopted the name John, which his brother officers thought rather more suitable.

Territorial units trained on 'drill nights', usually one evening a week, at weekends, and at a fortnight's annual camp. In Fig. 31 we see the Queen's Westminster Rifles marching at attention as they leave Yaverland Camp on the Isle of Wight in July 1909, during their annual camp. The battalion had become 16/London Regiment (Queen's Westminster Rifles) in April that year on the creation of the Territorial Force, which swept militia, volunteers and *Fig. 31*

Fig. 32
(previous
pages) yeomanry together in a unified second-line army. Private soldiers and junior NCOs are wearing khaki drill uniforms with the 1903 bandolier equipment, and carry the long Lee-Enfield rifle 'at the trail' as was traditional in a rifle regiment, rather than sloped on the shoulder. The captain marching at their head has an old-fashioned stand-up collar, and his 1897 pattern sword is carried at the slope. Its straight, rigid blade was ideal for thrusting. Officers took their swords to war in 1914. Some carried them at Neuve Chapelle in March 1915. Army Order 68 of June 1915 at last recognised that infantry officers would not carry swords in action, but at least one brave soul wore his on 1 July 1916 so that the lads could pick him out.

In 1914 a very high proportion of the Queen's Westminsters volunteered for foreign service, and the battalion (now called 1/Queen's Westminsters, as it had been split away from the new second-line 2/Queen's Westminsters, composed of men who had not volunteered or were not yet fit enough to go abroad) went to France that November. From early 1916 it was part of 56th (1st London) Division, in which it was brigaded with 2nd London Regiment, the London Rifle Brigade and Queen Victoria's Rifles. On 1 July 1916 it mounted the diversionary assault on Gommecourt, on the northern end of the Somme battlefront, losing twenty-eight officers and 475 riflemen of the twenty-eight and 661 who had gone into action.

The casualties suffered by units like the Queen's Westminsters gave the lie to pre-war sneers that 'Saturday night soldiers' would be no use if war came. Part of the animus against Territorials sprang from the fact that the civilian-turned-warrior was always an easy target for cartoonists or humorists: we always giggle at Captain Mainwaring and Sergeant Wilson. Part came from the fears of those who argued that conscription was the real answer to the military problems facing Britain even before 1914. The Territorials were, as so often throughout their history, a means of generating extra military manpower without paying what it was really worth. When war came their performance surprised many of their pre-war detractors.

The first Territorial battalion into action was the London Scottish, which fought on Messines Ridge, just south of Ypres, in August 1914. The battalion lost 321 of its 750 officers and men in its first battle. Paul Maze's photograph in Fig. 32 (*previous pages*) shows a group of survivors. Their purplish 'hodden-grey' kilts are generally concealed by greatcoats, and some wear woollen 'cap-comforters'. The authenticity of this shot is not marked out simply by the post-combat scruffiness of a proverbially smart unit, but by the fact that many soldiers are carrying cloth bandoliers. Boxed rifle ammunition arrived pre-loaded in these bandoliers, with two five-round clips to each of their five pouches, enabling it to be carried and distributed easily. The 'Piccadilly Highlanders' rose above their harsh introduction to war, and were a proverbially reliable battalion in a good division. Fig. 33 shows them going up the line in 1917. Some of their pipers wear 'SB' stretcher-bearers' brassards, and most soldiers seem to have a regimental feather hackle tucked into the hessian scrim on their helmets.

If upmarket Territorial battalions like the London Scottish or the LRB were an exception, 4/Queen's Royal Regiment (West Surrey) was more typical. It was one of the two Territorial battalions of the Queen's, and had its head-quarters in Mitcham Road, Croydon, which, a century on, is still a Territorial *Fig. 33*

Fig. 34

Army centre. In Fig. 34 we see it marching out of its barracks on mobilisation on 5 August 1914, commanded by Lieutenant Colonel Frank Watney, of the prominent local brewing family (the mounted officer on the left), with Major Utten Hooke as his second-in-command. Like other Territorial battalions it split: 1/4th Queen's spent the war in India; 2/4th spent much of its life in Britain, leaving for France in 1918; and 3/4th, commanded by Utten Hooke, now a lieutenant colonel, went to France in 1917. He was killed by shellfire near Arras on 21 June 1917 at the age of thirty-six, after less than a month in the field, leaving a widow in Croydon, and is buried in Level Crossing Cemetery at Fampoux. His successor lasted until October, by which time the battalion had been badly knocked about at Third Ypres. It was disbanded in early 1918, and its officers and men posted off to bring other units up to strength.

The Special Reserve was the final element of Haldane's creation. It had much in common with the old militia, for it tended to recruit soldiers who would have fitted comfortably into the ranks of regular regiments, and officers who had much in common with their regular counterparts and who, indeed, often used the Special Reserve as a way of obtaining a first commission which could then be translated into a regular commission. This latter facility had existed with the militia, and both Field Marshal Sir John French, commander-in-chief of the BEF in 1914, and his vice-chief of staff, the future Field Marshal Sir Henry Wilson, had gained their commissions through the militia. Men enlisted in the Special Reserve for six years, and began with six months' full-time training on regular army rates of pay, and three or four weeks of annual training thereafter. Special Reserve battalions, usually the third battalions of most county regiments, were based at the regiment's depot, generally in one of those red-brick barracks – like Stourton Barracks in Guildford, Le Marchant Barracks in Devizes, or Roussillon Barracks in Chichester – that had been built in the 1880s to accommodate the regiments created by Secretary of State Cardwell's reform of the army's structure. They had a small regular staff, and it was intended that on mobilisation Special Reserve officers and men would be posted to regular battalions of the same regiment.

In 1914 the Hampshire Regiment (which was to gain royal status in 1946) had two regular battalions, a Special Reserve battalion and six Territorial units, one rejoicing in the title 8th (Princess Beatrice's Isle of Wight Rifles) Battalion. Its regimental depot was at Lower Barracks in Winchester. In Fig. 35 we see its *Fig. 35*

Special Reservists marching into the city in September 1907. The inhabitants have hung out a banner to emphasise their approval of a regiment which was one of the only three line infantry units to draw more than 70 per cent of its recruits from its own area. The men are marching at ease: once called up to attention, they would carry their rifles at the slope, and pay attention to 'covering and dressing', so as to be properly aligned within ranks and files.

In contrast, Fig. 36 shows the Hampshires' depot commander (seated centre), his own staff and the district recruiting staff during the war. Herbert Graham Westmorland had been commissioned into the Isle of Wight Rifles in 1881 and transferred to the regular army in 1883. Promoted major in 1904, he had left the service in 1911, but was recalled in 1914 and appointed temporary lieutenant colonel to command the depot. Those in the
Fig. 36 photograph include Hampshires, with the star-shaped cap badge worn by

the regiment's officers (soldiers wore a cat-and-cabbage very similar to that of the York and Lancasters), on the staff of the depot. Some, from their medal ribbons, seem to have spent time at the front, while others show no sign of having been there yet.

Most of the recruiting staff sport the red collar tabs (properly called 'gorget patches') then worn by all general staff officers, regardless of rank. These had originally been introduced when the army proposed to have a 'blue ribbon' general staff, open only to officers who attended the staff college at Camberley, and were intended to identify trained staff officers in much the same way that the double carmine trouser-stripe marked out officers of the German general staff. Although the idea of an exclusive general staff soon perished, collar tabs remained, worn in red by the general staff, with some other variations, like the maroon tabs worn by medical staff and green by intelligence staff. Officers entitled to tabs also wore bands of the same colour round their service dress caps. The concept may have had sensible origins, but it helped emphasise the gap between staff officers and their regimental brothers in arms. Although, as we shall see later, senior officers and their staff were at risk in battle zones, the myth of the comfortably-housed staff, emerging only to ask fatuous questions or issue impracticable orders, became deeply entrenched, and 'the red badge of funk' did not help.

In the summer of 1914 it was evident to Lord Kitchener, snatched from the boat which was to have taken him back to govern Egypt to be Secretary of State for War, that the war would not be over by Christmas, and that in order to win it Britain would need to expand her army on an unprecedented scale. On 11 August he issued a proclamation calling for 100,000 volunteers between the ages of nineteen and thirty, repeating the process several times thereafter. The recruits who answered his call became part of the New Armies, often called Kitchener's Armies. Their battalions were numbered in regimental sequence after Territorial battalions, and their formal titles indicated their New Army status. However, many were raised from specific areas, or appealed to young men from similar backgrounds. Thus 11th (Service) Battalion the Welsh Regiment was known as the Cardiff Pals, and 16th (Service) Battalion the Middlesex Regiment as the Public Schools Battalion.

Fig. 37

Kitchener had a poor regard for the Territorials, and bypassed their County Associations to raise the New Armies through the adjutant-general's branch at the War Office. However, he was hugely successful in raising men: on 3 September 33,000 volunteered, a daily total never exceeded. Fig. 37 shows the Central London Recruiting Office, in Great Scotland Yard, just off Whitehall, with crowds of men waiting quietly in the rain to enlist. It is not simply that the sheer number is striking, but the varied headgear – from cloth cap to bowler and boater – demonstrates that men from a variety of backgrounds were proposing to sign on as private soldiers. The army suddenly attracted middle-class men in search of adventure as well as the respectable working class, and fathers of families who had much to leave behind.

In 1914 Norman Booth was thirty-two, and a carter for the Brighouse Co-operative Society. A pre-war photograph (Fig. 38) shows him in the second row, second from left, bowler-hatted and every inch the respectable working man. He was married to Eliza Jane and they had three children, Henry, Arnold and Ethel. As soon as war broke out he joined the 10th (Service) Battalion the York and Lancaster Regiment. Army life seems to have agreed with him: he told Ethel that they had rock buns for tea, and added that he would not have been given a responsible job in the battalion if he did not pay attention to his duties, urging her to study hard at school. Writing in a big round hand, he told her that his camp in south-east England was

a lovely place . . . I wish you could just see it heather all round and blackberries to be had for the picking but when you get older you may have the chance I hope so anyway wishing you many happy returns of the day from your loving DAD xxxxxx

His battalion, part of 21st Division, attacked between the villages of Fricourt and Mametz on 1 July 1916. A comrade wrote in his diary that:

The order came down to 'fix bayonets, you have got to fight for it lads.' We obeyed the order like men. And was soon out of the trench. I was running across a trench when the grid [wooden bridge] broke and let me through. I scrambled up and ran after the other boys . . .

Fig. 38

Fig. 39

Private Booth survived the first phase of the Somme, which cost his battalion 328 casualties. On 15 November, at the very end of the battle, he was reported missing, believed killed, and is commemorated on the Thiepval memorial. His papers in the Liddle Collection include his heartbreaking letters to Ethel, and a photograph (Fig. 39) of his wife and children, with a note saying that 'All these clothes were made by Ethel Booth.'

Walter Tull was less typical. He was a footballer, who had joined first-division Tottenham Hotspur in 1909 and transferred to the Southern League's Northampton Town in 1911. He was also black, the grandson of a slave: his father had arrived in Kent from Barbados in 1876 and married a local girl. His mother died in 1895, and his stepmother could not cope with six children so Walter and his brother Edward were sent to a Methodist orphanage in London. He became an apprentice printer when he left school, and a professional footballer after a brilliant 1908–09 season with the east London amateur club Clapton. Walter Tull joined 16/Middlesex, became a sergeant and fought on the Somme. Although there was a rule preventing 'any Negro or person of colour' from being granted a commission, in 1917 it was agreed that an individual 'not of pure European descent' could indeed be commissioned if he had been recommended by his CO and served with credit in the field. This followed the case of Reginald Collins, a civil servant in the West

Indies, who came close to being denied a commission on the grounds of his colour, but was eventually commissioned into the West India Regiment.

Tull was sent off to the Officer Cadet Battalion at Gailes in Ayrshire, and commissioned into the Middlesex Regiment in May 1917: Fig. 40 shows him every inch the jaunty subaltern. After serving on the Italian Front, where he was mentioned in dispatches, Tull returned to the Western Front, and on 25 March 1918 was hit leading an attack at Favreuil near Arras. Such was his popularity that his men made several attempts, under heavy fire, to bring him in. Walter Tull, the first black officer in a British regiment, is commemorated on the Arras Memorial to the Missing.

Tull had been commissioned after serving four and a half months in a Cadet Battalion, the norm for all officers granted temporary commissions after February 1916. Until then many had simply been commissioned direct from civil life, though service in an OTC certainly helped the process; from warrant officer or senior NCO rank in the regular army (the former Regimental Sergeant Major of 2/Royal Welch Fusiliers complained that becoming a second lieutenant had brought him down in the world); or through a Territorial 'class battalion' like the Artists' Rifles or Inns of Court Regiment, where there were many suitable young men. In 1914 the Artists' Rifles sent off fifty temporary officers still dressed as private soldiers, but with the addition of a single bronze star on each shoulder. Both Sandhurst (infantry and cavalry) and Woolwich (artillery and engineers) turned out regular officers during the war, and a number of temporary officers took regular commissions, although the fact that they had to relinquish any temporary rank and start as second lieutenants discouraged some potential transferees. In all, about half the 220,000 first

Fig. 40

commissions granted during the war went to men who had served in the ranks. Some of these were indeed 'genuine' rankers, men who would not have had the least prospect of gaining a commission in peacetime, while others were very similar – by background and education – to pre-war regular officers.

There were twenty-one infantry officer cadet battalions by the end of 1918, together with other cadet units which provided temporary officers for the artillery, engineers and cavalry. Officer cadets wore open-collared officer-style tunics with no badges of rank (NCOs and warrant officers removed their badges on arrival), and some cadets, like the majority of those in Fig. 41, a 1917 photograph of B Company, No. 20 Officer Cadet Battalion, bore the number of their battalion in Roman numerals in lieu of a cap badge. Robert Graves of 2/Royal Welch Fusiliers was an instructor at No. 4 Officer Cadet Battalion at Oxford in mid-1917, and thought that rugger and soccer were useful in identifying the right sort: 'Those who played rough, but not dirty, and had quick reactions, were the sort we needed, and we spent most of our spare time playing games with them.'

Fig. 41

Company Sergeant Major Ernest Shephard of 1/Dorsets, a pre-war regular, went to GHQ Cadet School at Blendecques near St-Omer in September 1916. He enjoyed his time there, finding it remarkable that such a diverse group, from private to RSM, pulled together so well. Commissioned into his beloved Dorsets, he was killed in temporary command of a company of 1/5th Dorsets in early 1917. He is buried in the AIF Burial Ground, Grass Lane, Flers, not far from Lieutenant Colonel the Earl of Feversham. Feversham had served in France as a yeomanry officer, but then went home to raise 21st (Service) Battalion the King's Royal Rifle Corps (Yeoman Rifles) from farming communities in Yorkshire, Northumberland and Durham, and was killed leading his battalion in its first attack in September 1916. Shephard was devoted to his profession, but much enjoyed a 'ramsammy' (army Indian for 'wild party') in the sergeants' mess, and came from the old army's 'us and them' world. Feversham was a substantial landowner in North Yorkshire, and had been a Conservative MP for ten years until he inherited his earldom. One of his corporals wrote that however much folk might scoff at the aristocracy, it took real character for a man to abandon Duncombe Park to die in the mud.

Men who joined the army were first given a medical, frequently by civilian medical practitioners who were not always rigorous in applying the standards. This often had less to do with simple incompetence or the desire to take on as many men as possible regardless of fitness, than with the fact that the army was geared to enlisting around 30,000 men a year, and the system simply collapsed under the weight of numbers. Medical standards changed during the war, and it was perfectly possible for a volunteer to be rejected in 1914 but to be passed fit for service in the infantry overseas in 1918. In 1914, 44 per cent of recruits could not attain the minimum expanded chest size of thirty-six inches, an index of the poor physical state of the urban working class.

A potential recruit who passed his medical was then attested. He held the Bible and swore, in the presence of a commissioned officer or justice of the peace, that he would 'honestly and faithfully defend His Majesty King George the Fifth in Person, Crown and Dignity against all enemies', and would also

Fig. 42

'observe and obey the orders of all generals and officers' set over him. Fig. 42 comes from a sequence showing the same officer and the same recruits from different angles. The officer wears lieutenant's badges on his cuffs and staff tabs on his collar, and the fact that he is walking with the aid of a crutch suggests that he has already been wounded too badly to serve at the front. The sergeant has the 'rootie gong', the Long Service and Good Conduct medal, which received white edges to its crimson ribbon in 1917, and the officer the 1914–15 Star, awarded from 1917, both of which mean that it is wrong to attribute the photograph, as some do, to 1914. The recruits have done their best for the occasion, but most are wearing thin cotton jackets, worn shiny, and overalls, smartened up for the day with collar and tie. Many soldiers found that their uniforms were the first really robust clothes they had ever worn.

The visual transformation from civilian to soldier was accomplished by the issue of uniform. 1914 volunteers often had to wait months or even years before they received their khaki, and many received the cordially detested 'Kitchener Blue' at the beginning of their service. Fig. 43 shows a group from a New Army battalion of the Gloucestershire Regiment. Most of the front row are wearing emergency blue uniforms, and almost all have the long-obsolete whitened Slade-Wallace equipment and the Lee-Metford rifle, replaced by the Short Magazine Lee-Enfield from 1903 but used as a stopgap (along with a variety of other weapons, including Japanese Arisakas) in 1914.

When khaki did appear, it consisted of a woollen serge tunic with a high stand-and-fall collar and four pockets, trousers made of the same material, long white drawers and a long-sleeved vest, with a 'greyback' collarless shirt with metal buttons: this was so long that it could be worn on its own without risk of embarrassing disclosures. Woollen puttees, each nine feet long, were wrapped around the lower leg, connecting trouser to boot, and tied off with an attached cotton ribbon. Infantry wore them wound from ankle to knee and mounted men (like the owner of the disembodied leg in Fig. 2, page 14) from knee to ankle. Men found them infuriating and unwieldy to start with, and on active service soldiers often wrapped empty sandbags round their puttees to prevent them from getting muddy: the practice was as frequently condemned as ignored. Ammunition boots were made of thick reversed hide and had leather laces. Their leather soles were hobnailed, and skidded remorselessly on cobbled roads.

Fig. 43

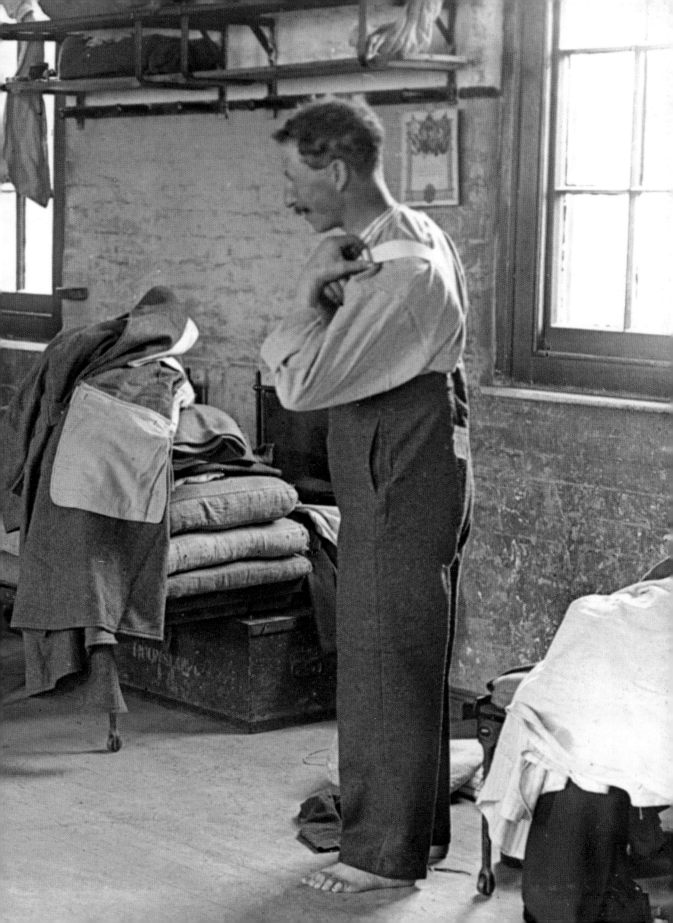

Fig. 44
(previous
pages)

Brass shoulder titles were worn from the beginning of the war, and as the conflict went on divisional and brigade arm patches were added to the tunic. By 1918 a seasoned observer, looking at a soldier, could tell not simply what regiment he was in, but what division he served with, whether he had been decorated (medal ribbons above the left pocket); wounded (wound stripes – a gold bar on the left cuff for each wound); how long he had been out (overseas service stripes on his right cuff); how long he had served in the army (inverted chevrons on his left cuff); and whether he was a specialist of any sort: signallers wore crossed flags on their left sleeve, Lewis gunners an encircled LG within a laurel wreath, and so on.

When he first drew his kit, though, the recruit was presented with unpressed, dusty-smelling khaki (Fig. 44, *previous pages*) and a tangle of equipment which required blanco-ing (if webbing) and polishing (if leather). Within units the issue and maintenance of uniform, weapons and equipment was the responsibility of the quartermaster. British Army quartermasters were traditionally commissioned from the ranks, usually having just served their time as RSM of a regular unit, and were proverbially full of sin and experience.

Fig. 45, taken just before the war, shows the quartermaster of a battalion of King's Own Scottish Borderers standing with the regimental quartermaster sergeant outside his office. The QM is wearing his regiment's Leslie tartan trews and a non-regulation pea-jacket. The RQMS's distinctive badge of rank was to be replaced, in 1913–14, by a wreathed crown on the cuff. This happened because infantry battalions went from having eight companies, each with a colour sergeant as its senior NCO, to four, each with a company sergeant major. Company sergeant majors became Warrant Officers Class 2 (the RSM, the most senior non-commissioned member of the unit, was a Warrant Officer Class 1), as did the RQMS. CSMs wore a plain crown on their cuffs; the RQMS added a wreath. This RQMS is taking the strain off his trews by wearing plain khaki trousers, though his tunic is in the traditional Scots doublet cut.

Not all quartermaster sergeants were steady old gentlemen who had grown grey over their ledgers. At the battle of Mons on 23 August 1914, RQMS Thomas Fitzpatrick of 2nd Royal Irish, acting without orders, extemporised a small force consisting of cooks, grooms and storemen and held a crucial

Fig. 45
(opposite)

crossroads at a critical moment. Awarded the DCM and commissioned, he was a lieutenant colonel at the war's end. The happiness of a battalion could depend almost as much on these worthies as upon its commanding officer: few units could succeed without a good quartermaster, though they were not always comfortable folk. When I look at this QM's face I am not sure that a young subaltern would have been wise to begin his request for some buckshee kit with a cheery cry of 'What-ho, Quarters!'

Although men flocked to the colours in huge numbers, with 1,200,000 joining by December 1914 and an average of 100,000 a month in early 1915, it was evident that there were practical limits to the voluntary system. Accepting men below regulation height into 'Bantam' battalions, a process which began with 15/ and 16/Cheshire in 1914, enabled some sturdy men to serve their country, but there were soon practical difficulties. Finally, in December 1916 the commander of the 35th (Bantam) Division warned that his division had become a repository for men who were not simply undersized, but were 'physically undeveloped and unfit men of a low moral standard', and the enlistment of Bantams was suspended.

In the summer of 1915 the National Registration scheme required men and women aged fifteen to sixty-five to register their details. The particulars of men aged eighteen to forty-one were transferred to a pink form, and those in essential war work ('starred occupations') had a star stamped on their form. The process revealed that there were 3,400,000 men theoretically available for military service. The Derby Scheme, named for Lord Derby, Director of Recruiting, strove to persuade these men to register voluntarily for call-up in age-banded groups, with married men forming separate groups, which were to be called up last.

The Derby Scheme was only a qualified success: overall about half the target population failed to register, and in early 1916 Parliament passed the first Military Service Act, authorising the call-up of single men aged eighteen to forty-one. Of the Derby men summoned perhaps a third did not report for duty, often because details in the National Register were inaccurate. The government responded by passing a second Military Service Act, which increased the liability for military service and enabled the recall of ex-soldiers whose enlistment period had expired. The first conscripts reached the front in the middle of the Somme battle. James Dunn complained that while 'the average physique was good enough', there were too many men with 'narrow or misshapen chests, and other deformities and defects'. A good number had received less than six weeks' training, fired only five live rounds, and could neither load their rifles nor fix and unfix bayonets.

Conscription, never before employed in modern British history, raised serious issues of civil liberties, not least in the case of those who objected to military service on moral grounds. Those who raised conscientious objections to military service were given the option of serving in non-combatant units, but a small minority of absolutists – who would neither wear uniform nor obey orders – were repeatedly sentenced to terms of imprisonment with hard labour. Although there was a widespread anti-'conchie' feeling amongst serving soldiers, it was hard for even the most hostile to criticise the Friends' Ambulance Unit, composed of Quakers who would not bear arms but served with marked courage at the front.

The casualties of 1916 encouraged the government to introduce a third Military Service Act in April 1917, which seized more men from industry and enabled re-examination of those who had earlier failed medicals. In May 1917 the whole training process was rationalised so that young conscripts would serve in Young Soldiers battalions and then Graduated battalions until they were old enough to be sent to France. In the last two years of the war the army was conscripting eighteen-year-olds at one extreme and married men in their fifties at the other. Frank Gray, a thirty-seven-year-old lawyer, was driven to the depot by his chauffeur to begin his infantry training in 1917, and though he found the training hard and the entire military system antiquated, he retained great affection for his commanding officer, who was 'humane, kind and courageous'. At the other extreme young Fred Hodges and his friends had worked hard to get fit before they were called up. By the summer of 1918 half of the British soldiers in France were eighteen-year-olds, their youth poignantly underlined by both contemporary photographs and the headstones in the cemeteries which mark the British line of advance in the war's last victorious hundred days. Of the sixty-four burials at Haspres Copse cemetery, not far from Cambrai, fifty are from 19/Lancashire Fusiliers, who fought nearby on 13 October. The oldest, at forty, is Private Charles

Fig. 46

Wolsoncroft: most of the rest are in their teens and early twenties. By 1918 old Tom was very rare, and young Tommy very common indeed.

Just as the enlistment of so many men encouraged women to join the civilian workforce – there was a 25 per cent increase in working women by 1918, to over six million, about 950,000 of them in munitions factories – so the shortage of manpower encouraged the government to put women into uniform. The Women's Auxiliary Army Corps was founded in early 1917, and almost 57,000 women had served in it by the Armistice. The military authorities were reluctant to grant its members full military status, so they were enrolled and not enlisted, and had officials rather than officers, forewomen not sergeants, assistant forewomen instead of corporals, and workers rather than privates. They were employed as clerks, telephonists, cooks and drivers: Fig. 46 shows some drivers outside their quarters in Calais. A few were gasmask instructors, as were some officers of the much smaller Women's Royal Naval Service: Fig. 47 shows a member of the WRNS training male soldiers on the 'small box' respirator. About 6,000 members of the WAAC served in France: the two girls in Fig. 48 are using German steel helmets to collect their day's rations. In 1918 an official inquiry into reports of their allegedly loose morals established that only

*Fig. 47
(opposite
top)*

*Fig. 48
(opposite
bottom)*

Fig. 49

twenty-one had become pregnant, and just thirty-seven had been sent home from France for misconduct.

By the time the WAAC arrived in France that most idiosyncratic of units, the First Aid Nursing Yeomanry, had been there for over three years. The part-time, volunteer FANY had been formed in 1907 by an officer who had served in the Boer War, and it was initially intended to contain skilled horsewomen who could hurtle onto the battlefield to administer first aid to the wounded. The first FANYs, operating with a predictable absence of official support, reached France in October 1914, and for the rest of the war they helped in hospitals, drove trucks and ambulances, and ran an assortment of canteens: no fewer than seventeen of them earned the Military Medal. Fig. 49 shows a group of ambulance drivers in long goatskin coats in early 1917. Although historians often focus on the role of 'munitionettes' (especially the 'canaries' whose skin was dyed yellow by chemicals used in shells) in highlighting the wartime role of women, for soldiers at the front the visible embodiment of self-assured women, pushing out into what had traditionally been male jobs, drove ambulances under fire or served tea and buns within artillery range of the front line and, as we shall see later, nursed broken bodies and shattered minds.

3

Steel and Fire

The war came at a time of accelerating change. The Franco–Prussian War of 1870–71 was the first in which breech-loading rifles were used by the infantry of both sides, and by the turn of the century all major armies were equipped with magazine-fed rifles and quick-firing field guns. Smokeless powder propelled rifle bullets and artillery shells, and high explosive, developed in the 1880s, furnished the bursting charge in shells. These could now be spun off to longer ranges than ever before, greatly increasing the battlefield's lethal depth. The heavy machine gun, mounted on a tripod or a sledged carriage, firing rifle-calibre ammunition, housed in a fabric belt, through a barrel cooled by a water-filled jacket, was in service across much of the world.

Killing power had increased exponentially over the past fifty years. Armies saw that battlefields drenched by a swelling volume of fire would present their soldiers with very serious difficulties, not least because, as the French thinker Ardant du Picq (himself killed in 1870) had observed, cohesion under fire had traditionally depended on discipline, imposed from above, and emulation, generated within the combat group. If men took cover and spread out, then 'cohesion will no longer have the sanction of mutual surveillance'. After 1870–71 there was indeed a tendency to train infantry to spread out and advance in rushes. The British, with their sharp experience of Boer rifle-fire in South Africa in 1899–1902, took marksmanship increasingly seriously, and went to war in 1914 with the most sombre and practical uniforms in Europe.

However, by 1914 even the British had come to share the conviction, held by French allies and German opponents, that, as *Infantry Training 1914* put it:

'The main essential in battle is to close with the enemy, cost what it may.' It went on, adding emphasis in bold type, to affirm that artillery, machine-gun and rifle fire should be used '*to bring such a superiority of fire to bear on the enemy as to make the advance to close quarters possible*'. Once local commanders were confident that they had won the fire-fight, they would order

> the *charge* to be sounded, the call will at once be taken up by all buglers, and all neighbouring units will join the charge as quickly as possible. During the delivery of the assault the men will cheer, bugles be sounded, and pipes played.

The development of tactics throughout the war focused on this relationship between fire and shock. The proliferation of weapons like light machine guns, trench mortars and grenades, along with the development of the tank and the ground-attack aircraft, allowed fire and manoeuvre to become simultaneous rather than merely sequential. In 1914 training manuals described an assault delivered by brave men pressing in to assert their moral superiority over an enemy shaken by their fire. By 1918 there was widespread recognition that

Fig. 50

although artillery played a crucial role in shaping the battlefield, isolating the sector under attack, mauling reinforcements on their way forward, and physically degrading the enemy's defences, its effect on the defender's mind was scarcely less significant than that on his body. Instead of the long bombardments of the early years of the war, which inevitably compromised surprise and confronted the attacker with a wilderness of his own making, short, sharp firestorms blazed through the full depth of an enemy's position. By 1918 attackers, their disposition linear at the start of the war, were using a variety of formations ('worms' was a graphic description) which sought not so much the intact surfaces of the enemy's defence as the gaps between them.

Communications had not kept pace with killing power, and this simple fact had a profound effect on tactics and training. Although the British had been slower than some other armies to recognise the military potential of the telephone, they used it very widely during the war. With overhead cables it provided communications between major headquarters and back to the United Kingdom. These wires required constant maintenance and repair, even without damage inflicted by the enemy. In Fig. 50 we see linesmen of the Royal Engineers Signal Service (there was no independent Corps of Signals until just after the war) repairing the line west of Ypres in the particularly hard winter of 1917, when the weight of snow on the line compounded their problems. Closer to the front, overhead or surface-laid cables were vulnerable to both shellfire and accident, so important cables were buried, and as we can see in Fig. 51 were often shrouded in hardened ducts to improve resistance to shelling. In 1915 they were placed two or three feet underground, and from 1916 the six-foot bury was in general use. The blue-and-white brassard of the RE Signal Service is clearly visible.

Fig. 51

Even so, it was impossible to guarantee that telephones would work during a battle, for a wise enemy would try to hit nodal points with shells fused to burst below the surface. In the front line itself it was often a matter of luck as to whether communications survived in action. The infantry ration party in Fig. 52 is taking 'hay boxes', containers of hot food, up a communication trench in 1917, and the cables on the left of the picture, looped above the trench on a barbed-wire picket, are not likely to last for long, even though they might well provide the vital link between a battalion's forward companies in the front-line trench and its headquarters and reserve a short distance behind. Nevertheless, there were times when communications outlasted the battle. Lieutenant Colonel Wilfrith Elstob, commanding 16/Manchester on Manchester Hill just west of St-Quentin on 21 March 1918, was able to assure his brigade commander over the

Fig. 52

telephone, via a well-buried cable, that the position would be held to Fig. 53 the last. He rang off to die, revolver in hand, as the Germans overran his headquarters.

Trench warfare was neither new to the First World War (it had been used in the American Civil War and was a feature of the Russo–Japanese War of 1904–05) nor the dominating feature on all fronts. Before the war in France went to earth in the early autumn of 1914, and rather more often in both Mesopotamia and Palestine, signallers needed to lay cable quickly, and here one of the war's most distinctive pieces of equipment came into its own. The cable wagon was drawn by a team of four horses, and its seven-man detachment could lay cable at the gallop. In Fig. 53 a cable wagon is crossing a river in Mesopotamia alongside a damaged bridge, and some of its detachment have stripped to help their vehicle across. Signallers had to master semaphore (whose flags were the origin of the qualification badge on their left sleeve) and the heliograph, and both were used to send signals in Morse code

Fig. 54

even on the Western Front, and rather more often elsewhere. Fig. 54, a photograph taken by Ernest Brooks at the time of King George V's visit to the front in September 1916, shows a prominent hill near Fricourt on the Somme being used as a heliograph repeating station, with a signaller and observer working as a team. The emblem on the sign is the red rose of 55th (West Lancashire) Division. 'They win or die,' affirmed the division's slogan, 'who wear the rose of Lancashire.'

Battery-powered signal lamps could be used when the sun failed to oblige, as it so often did in north-west Europe. Fig. 55, one of a sequence showing 13/Durham Light Infantry preparing to assault Veldhoek in the Ypres salient in

August 1917, shows one signaller busy with a lamp. Another, his helmet scrimmed with camouflaged hessian, uses a telescope to read flashes from a forward position, doubtless awaiting, with grim anticipation, the flashed order to move up.

As the war went on there were further developments. Mounted

Fig. 55

88

dispatch riders had long been a feature of war, and in 1914 the army appealed for experienced motorcyclists who owned their own machines. The call was enthusiastically answered, for the most part by middle-class young men. Hayden Foster of Darlington found himself given £62.10s for his bike, which then became War Office property, and, like his fellow volunteers, was appointed a corporal in the Royal Engineers. Many volunteer dispatch riders subsequently gained commissions, and Foster was no exception. He became a second lieutenant in the Darlington-raised 151 Heavy Battery RGA, and earned a Military Cross when, as a forward observation officer (FOO), he rallied a party of leaderless infantry and fought off a counter-attack. He survived the war. Dispatch riders were even more important in theatres of war where distances were vast, terrain difficult and telephones rare. Fig. 56 shows a dispatch rider on an improvised bridge in East Africa.

Fig. 56

Fig. 57

Carrier pigeons, seen feeding at their loft (usually located in the area of divisional headquarters) in Fig. 57, were carried by attacking troops, whose officers were issued with pre-written message forms which required only simple addition or deletion before being clipped to the pigeon's leg and winged away. By 1917 it took an average of twenty-five minutes to get a message by pigeon from the front to its loft. There were over 20,000 carrier pigeons in France by 1918, with 90,000 men trained to handle them. Fig. 58, depicting a

Fig. 58

pigeon being released from an armoured port in a tank, is a perfect illustration of the way in which the war often combined ancient and modern. It was soon clear that it was unwise to rely on any single means of communication, and by 1916 the power-buzzer, which could transmit Morse code by way of a powerful vibrator, the klaxon horn and the DD electric lamp were amongst the methods used to supplement pigeon and telephone.

One of the problems with telephones and buzzers was that they used a single line for their transmissions and had an earth return, and so, in the words of one authority: 'The earth was . . . alive with buzzer and telephone induction.' The Germans listened in to British transmissions, and security was often compromised. In October 1915 Captain A.C. Fuller of the Royal Engineers Signal Service devised the first Fullerphone, a portable DC line Morse telegraph which was almost impossible to overhear but which could be used simultaneously with telephone conversation down a normal line. An improved version was used in the Second World War. Fig. 59 shows a Fullerphone in a shell-hole with three soldiers wearing the first model of the 'small box' respirator: the box containing air-cleansing chemicals is in the canvas bag on their chests.

Fig. 59

The photograph is too good to be true. Fig. 60, another shot in the same sequence (in the Royal Signals Museum at Blandford), shows the three men poised, this time in a gas-free environment, to repel an assault. The soldier on the left, his armband clear in one of the photographs and his RE shoulder title visible here, is from the Royal Engineers Signal Service. The man in the centre is a driver in the Royal Field Artillery, and the man working the Fullerphone is in the Royal Garrison Artillery. This is a posed sequence, with the Fullerphone as star of the show.

A few wireless sets, cumbersome and unreliable, had gone to France with the BEF in 1914, and by 1918 their successors were widely used on all fronts. They remained of limited value on the battlefield itself, partly because it took some time to make them small enough to be easily man-packed. Their valves made them fragile, and some relied upon bulky and vulnerable accumulators which required frequent recharging. Most used Morse code rather than voice transmissions, and receivers and transmitters were generally separate. There were concerns about the visibility of aerials, skilled German radio direction-finding and, because procedures were still in their infancy, constant risks of breached

Fig. 60

Fig. 61

security. Nevertheless, the 'trench set' shown in a dugout in Fig. 61 worked well as a link between divisional and brigade headquarters in the static conditions of trench warfare, and by 1917–18 structures, procedures and technology had evolved sufficiently to make radio a real asset. The Australian signallers in Fig. 62 (their nationality visible from their sunburst collar-dogs) are using a set in the open towards the end of the war, but it is all too evidently not 'field hardened'. If radios were useful on the Western Front, they were invaluable in some other theatres of war. In Mesopotamia the beleaguered garrison of Kut al Amara depended on a single radio set, which sent 6,313 messages in the 144 days of the siege.

Fig. 62

The closer to the front, the less reliable communications became. On the battlefield officers used verbal orders, whistles, or simple messages sent by runners. To lead effectively, by injecting their own personality into the battle, they had to go forward, where they found that their ability to communicate easily only with those within earshot immediately reduced their effectiveness. To command on anything but the most modest scale they were dragged back to a spot where they had access to telephone or radio. This was the real conundrum for battalion and brigade commanders, and it is one reason for the shockingly high losses suffered by officers holding both these appointments. Some 232 generals were killed or wounded on all fronts. Eight were wounded twice, and seventy-eight were killed, sixty-two of them on the Western Front. They met their deaths in a variety of ways, but the fact that they were, statistically, more likely to be killed by small-arms fire than were the men under their command, the overwhelming majority of whom were killed by artillery fire, suggests that going forward to lead, rather than staying back to command, was what killed them.

By 1918 the pamphlet *The Training and Employment of Divisions* decreed that: 'All infantry officers taking part in an attack must be dressed and equipped exactly the same as their men.' Some officers had in fact dressed just like their men, though with the addition of the appropriate badges of rank on their epaulettes, during the battle of the Somme in 1916, and by 1917 most had a Tommy's jacket to hand for front-line service. In Fig. 63 we see two

Fig. 63

infantry battalion commanders and their adjutants in a captured German communication trench on Messines Ridge on 11 June 1917. It is evidently quiet on that part of the front, between Second Army's capture of the ridge on 7 June and the beginning of Fifth Army's attack further north at the end of July. The fact that two officers are wearing shorts reminds us that there were bursts of hot weather even in the year of Passchendaele. The tousled CO has probably just returned from visiting his forward companies, and is evidently feeling the heat in his soldier's tunic. Hair oil was widely used by officers, who had an insatiable appetite for the Jermyn Street fripperies that somehow made life more bearable, though one Cameronian officer gave up wearing it when he found that it encouraged rats to nibble at his head.

In contrast, the brigadier general and his staff (from the 29th Division, which cut its teeth at Gallipoli before serving with distinction on the Western Front) in Fig. 64 look less comfortable. The rank of brigadier general was not substantive: unless an officer was promoted out of his brigadier's post, he *Fig. 64*

risked crashing back down to his permanent rank when he gave up the appointment. Typically, infantry brigades were led by officers who had commanded infantry battalions (or, less often, cavalry regiments) immediately beforehand. George William Grogan commanded an infantry brigade from the summer of 1918. On 29 May that year, still a lieutenant colonel, he earned the VC in a spectacular act of heroism, riding his horse right into the firing line (one charger was shot under him) and encouraging both British and French troops reeling under the impact of a German attack. Although Grogan's case was extreme, many brigadiers showed heroism and ran its attendant risks.

As he trudges forward, this officer will be reduced to communicating by runner, and at the mercy of a sniper who spots his red tabs and epaulettes. There were times when senior officers rendered their men the most useful service simply by staying alive, though all their soldierly instincts argued to the contrary. This brigadier general already has three wound stripes, and his brigade major on the left, chief of staff in modern parlance, has one. All four officers have their respirators in the 'ready' position, for gas was no respecter of rank.

There was a direct link between command, communications and training. As we have seen, the army expanded to an unprecedented degree. In the process it needed to produce large numbers of commanders, staff officers and special staff – like the fast-growing artillery staff. Most key command appointments were in the hands of regular officers, though some Territorials and a very few wartime-commissioned officers eventually rose to command brigades. Some officers were unavoidably promoted above the level of their competence, and had to adapt not simply to a level of command to which they could never have aspired in peacetime, but to ongoing changes in weapons and tactics. All, capable or not, had to cope with a training organisation which evolved but slowly. Deficiencies in training were largely remedied by experience, and though I recoil from the expression 'learning curve', there is truth in the argument that the army that emerged from the Somme understood combined arms tactics in a way that it had not done before.

British tendency to over-control, to be prescriptive rather than descriptive in the orders process, reflected the fact that, at least for the first two years of the war, commanders could neither assume high levels of knowledge amongst their subordinates, nor, because of the limited communications at their disposal,

Fig. 65

guarantee to intervene at the right moment. Perhaps the most important ingredient in the victorious advance of the last hundred days was the fact that most divisional and brigade commanders understood their jobs well enough to be able to generate purposeful activity in the absence of orders.

Any successful commander quickly came to understand that the indirect fire of artillery, in which guns engaged a target invisible from the gun-line, was a quintessential element of the war. In the advance, artillery FOOs would communicate with their guns by way of cable paid out from backpacked drums carried by the signallers who accompanied them, and in static defence they would generally use telephones already in situ. Fig. 65 shows an FOO signalling his guns by lamp from the top of a dugout: the fact that he is keeping a low profile suggests that this is a shot taken in action.

Fig. 66 (*overleaf*), showing FOOs of 12th Division on the edge of Cuthbert crater, two miles north-east of Arras, in April 1917, is far and away the best photograph of a gunner observation post. The pipe-smoking officer is using a periscope to minimise his exposure to sniper fire and shell fragments, and the signallers (badged Royal Field Artillery, for signalling *within* infantry battalions and their artillery equivalents was a regimental responsibility) are making the best of the cover offered by the crater. The photographer, too, is wisely keeping his head down. These officers are probably conducting a process called registration, in which likely targets were hit, usually by a process of 'establishing a bracket'. The observer would first bring exploratory shells

Fig. 66
(overleaf)

Fig. 67

onto the direct line between himself and the target. He would then place rounds beyond and in front of it (the bracket) until, by splitting the difference between successive shells, he was able to hit it. Experienced observers would do this confidently, with bold corrections, while the less accomplished would 'creep', making many time-consuming adjustments.

The ground had to be watched carefully so that adjustments were not made from another battery's shell. As a gun fired, a message would be relayed over the telephone. 'Shot one, twenty' meant that the right-hand gun in the battery had fired a shell which would be in the air for twenty seconds. The observer would know precisely when to expect the shell, and, warned that the right-hand gun had fired, would know that the rest of the battery's fire would fall to the left of the adjusting round. He could order 'individual corrections' to bring each gun in the battery onto precisely the same target, though the process was relatively complex. The details of each target were recorded at the gun position, and it could then be hit without the need for subsequent ranging. The target might form part of a barrage plan, or simply be a spot – like a road junction or ruined farm – that might require specific attention.

Height gave an observer a significant advantage, and the army went to war with a telescopic observation pole which was mounted on an artillery limber. In Fig. 67 we see an officer of 82nd Field Battery RFA controlling artillery fire during the advance on Kut al Amara in mid-1915. Although this device was not without its use in the flat terrain of Mesopotamia, it was of little value in static operations on the Western Front. However, camouflage experts were skilled at adapting local cover, often by substituting art for nature under cover of darkness: the tree in the forefront of Fig. 68 is artificial, and contains a ladder for the use of an FOO.

Fig. 68

Fig. 69

With the battle moving forward beyond the view of initial observation posts, FOOs would have to work from the high-water mark of the previous attack, usually accompanied by two signallers with drums of cable. It was dangerous work, for an FOO party formed an easily-identified group, constituting a high-value target for snipers and other gunners too. Fig. 69 shows an FOO party just behind a line of attacking infantry in Palestine, with the FOO on the left and his signaller, telephone handset in the satchel, on the right.

From September 1914 the British began to conduct artillery-fire control from aircraft, and later from observation balloons. In the latter case observers used a telephone line to speak to the guns, and in the former they first dropped messages marked with prominent streamers, and later used aircraft-mounted radios to transmit orders. Both sides made widespread use of captive balloons, hydrogen-filled envelopes with a wicker basket suspended below for the two-man crew. They were raised and lowed by power winches, and had to be pulled down rapidly if wind speed exceeded acceptable limits, or if they were attacked by enemy aircraft.

Balloon crewmen were trained at the Royal Flying Corps' kite balloon school at Roehampton and, unlike other aircrew, were equipped with parachutes. Parachuting from a blazing balloon was a risky business, because chunks of blazing gas-bag sometimes fell faster than parachutes. Captain Basil Hallam Radford, who had popularised the song 'Gilbert the Filbert', died in 1916 when his balloon broke loose from its moorings. The officer with him jumped to safety, but Radford became detached from his parachute and fell like a stone. In Fig. 70 an Australian kite balloon is being successfully inflated: if the process was not carried out correctly, the hydrogen rushed into one end of the gas-bag and the balloon, originating what has become a widely used phrase, 'went pear-shaped'. Several of the detachment are wearing the distinctive Royal Flying Corps tunic which buttoned right across the chest: its alleged similarity to a maternity smock helped make it unpopular.

Fig. 70

Fig. 71   Whether fire orders came from land or air, they were translated into usable data at the battery command post on the gun-line using a gridded table called an artillery board. Fig. 71 seems to be unique, and shows an often-forgotten link in the chain of artillery-fire control. This sergeant of the Royal Garrison Artillery's Lowland Heavy Battery, a Territorial unit based in Edinburgh, is transferring target information to his notebook. He is probably the detachment commander – No. 1 in gunner parlance – of one of the guns in his battery. Using information sent down by the FOO, the command post has calculated all the details required to enable his gun to hit a number of targets: data includes the 'switch angle' (the bearing to be set on the gun's dial sight), the 'angle of sight' (an adjustment to elevation to allow for the fact that gun and target might be at different heights) and the fuse setting (to regulate the time of burst of a shrapnel shell). This battery was 52nd (Lowland) Division's integral heavy battery, and went to war with the 4.7-inch gun,

discarded by regular batteries in favour of the more effective sixty-pounder, and replaced, even in Territorial batteries, by 1917.

The sixty-pounder, a Canadian-manned version of which is shown in Fig. 72, had come into service in 1905 and was the standard equipment for the four-gun heavy battery which was then an integral part of each regular division. At its lightest it weighed in at almost five tons, just within the capacity of animal traction, though it took eight heavy horses to haul each gun. Heavy batteries initially had only four guns apiece, as opposed to the six of field and horse batteries. In mid-1916 heavy batteries on the Western Front were given six guns each, in recognition of the need for the increased centralisation of these heavy pieces.

This photograph was taken on 10 August 1918, two days after the beginning of the battle of Amiens marked what Ludendorff called 'the black day of the German army'. It shows how life on a gun-line was dominated by ammunition flow. The soldiers kneeling on the left are setting fuses. One has begun to move towards the gun with two bag-charges of cordite, which will be shoved into the weapon's breech once the shell has been rammed home.

Fig. 72

Shells lie ready just behind the freshly-turned earth where the spade at the end of the gun's trail is embedded in the ground. The weapon's elevation suggests that it is not firing at anything like its maximum range, which thanks to wartime refinement of ammunition had been extended from an initial 10,300 to 12,300 yards.

During the whole war over ten million rounds of sixty-pounder ammunition were expended on the Western Front alone. Most shells were yellow, with coloured bands denoting their filling. They arrived in the theatre of war without fuses, with either a flat or, to assist handling, a ringed nosecap. They were generally fused at an ammunition depot at a railhead behind the lines before being taken forward to the gun-line by a battery's wagons under *Fig. 73* cover of darkness. Fig. 73 shows two soldiers, almost certainly of the Army

Ordnance Corps, fitting fuses to shells. A notice, hanging at an angle, warns NCOs and men that they are not allowed at the dump unless working there, for the process was not without hazard, and men needed to concentrate on their task. Unfused projectiles were comparatively safe. The original caption for Fig. 74 maintains that these Army Ordnance Corps soldiers are fusing the 'toffee-apple' projectiles for trench mortars in September 1916 at Ovillers, just off the main Albert to Bapaume road. They are in fact playing cards on a copy of the *Daily Mail*, perhaps encouraged to do so by the photographer, for the newspaper had won the contract to reproduce and market selected images, which it did under the title *The Daily Mail Official War Postcards*. Such photographs were widely reproduced elsewhere, and their tone was deliberately sanitised: this is just the shot of jolly Tommy that the series specialised in.

It had been intended to supplement the sixty-pounder with even heavier weapons, but trials of the 9.2-inch siege howitzer, which hurled a 290-pound shell out to almost 14,000 yards, had only just been completed when war broke out. The prototype, named *Mother*, was in action near Neuve Chapelle, in French Flanders, in November 1914, and sixteen further weapons were ordered. The 9.2, seen seconds after firing in Fig. 75, weighed in at just under fourteen tons, and when in action had to be steadied by an earth box (just in front of the muzzle) weighing another eleven tons when filled. The gun and its carriage were broken down into three four-wheeled vehicles for transport, and a single Holt caterpillar tractor could haul the whole train. The heaviest weapons used by the British Army in the war were two fourteen-inch railway guns, *Boche Buster* and *Scene Shifter*, with a stupendous range of 38,000 yards.

The real workhorse of British artillery was the eighteen-pounder, which came into service in 1905 and initially fired only an air-burst shrapnel shell *Fig. 75* containing 375 lead balls weighing forty-one to the pound, blown from the

shell by a burster charge of black powder. A high-explosive shell was hurriedly brought into service in the autumn of 1914, and as the war went on successive improvements increased the gun's range from 6,525 yards to just over 9,000. It was a quick-firer, so-called because the shell was attached to a brass cartridge, and its recuperators absorbed most of the recoil as the barrel sprang back on firing and then pushed it forward again. A well trained six-man detachment could fire up to thirty rounds a minute.

Although the eighteen-pounder always suffered from the fact that its light projectile did little damage to trenches and, even when a quick-acting 106 fuse was introduced in late 1916, to wire either, it was reliable, handy and accurate. Its steel shield was intended to keep out rifle-fire, for it was designed at a time when direct fire was widely used, and gave good protection against both shrapnel and shell splinters. In Fig. 76 (*overleaf*) we see an eighteen-pounder in a camouflaged position south of Ypres on 19–20 October 1914. The setting is wholly authentic, with the gun in a 'semi covered' position, out of direct view of the enemy but with little to conceal its muzzle-flash. A 'covered' position would see it more deeply tucked into a fold in the ground, but this might make it hard for the shell to clear intervening crest-lines. One of the advantages of the howitzer, which could lob shells on a steeper angle, was that it could use crests for cover, and drop its shells on concealed enemy guns and field fortifications.

Here the gun's No. 1, a sergeant, kneels by the trail. The No. 3, just behind the breech, is the gun-layer, with his dial-sight visible above him. The No. 4, with a bandaged head-wound, is about to load a shell into the open breech. The No. 2, who works the breech, seems to have been hit, and lies partly out of sight to the low left. Nos 5 and 6 are busy extracting ammunition from the limber, with the one furthest from the camera setting fuses. But look more closely, and you will see that all are grinning: not the set rictus of determination, but the quiet snigger of a private joke. They are going through the motions for the photographer, and, with more serious work to hand, cannot take it wholly seriously. They are serious, old-army-start-of-war gunners. We can see that the RFA and RHA were proud of being mounted branches (the RGA was not), because the sergeant is wearing his spurs in Flanders mud.

Fig. 76 (overleaf)

Fig. 77   In contrast, Fig. 77 shows an eighteen-pounder in Carnoy Valley, near Montauban on the Somme, adding its sharp voice to the 'creeping barrage' fired during the attack on Pozières Ridge on 30 July 1916. The No. 4 is cradling the shell with his forearm, just as he has been taught, to avoid painful confrontation between fragile fingers and grimy metal. There is not a spur in sight. On the right is an officer in his dark khaki shirt, with a megaphone in his hand, ready to order the next change in elevation and bearing which will move the barrage, at least in theory, just ahead of the attacking infantry, at perhaps 100 yards in three minutes. Field guns usually engaged the enemy's infantry and placed a curtain of fire, moving or static as required, in front of their own. Medium and heavy guns sought to destroy fixed defences or reached out to smite opposing artillery in 'counter-battery' fire, a process assisted, as the war went on, by developments in things like flash-spotting and sound-ranging, and with their accuracy enhanced by improved survey and

mapping, and by increasing attention to meteorological conditions, which meant so much to the shell's spinning transit through the atmosphere.

Fig. 78 shows the result of counter-battery fire. This eighteen-pounder has taken a direct hit from a medium shell, probably a 5.9-inch, and is a total wreck: there can have been no hope for its detachment. Although only the thirteen-pounder, used by the Royal Horse Artillery, weighed less than the eighteen-pounder, even this comparatively handy weapon could get stuck. In Fig. 79 men haul on drag ropes to get an eighteen-pounder out of the mud of the Ypres salient

Fig. 78

in 1917. The gun's six-horse team stands ready behind the toiling gunners, awaiting the moment when the towing-eye on the gun's trail can be slipped over the hook on the limber, and horsepower can replace manpower.

Fig. 79

At the start of the war each British field gun had 1,000 rounds available in the theatre of war, spread out from the ready-to-use ammunition in the limber to reserve stock at base depots. During the preliminary bombardment for the Somme eighteen-pounder ammunition was topped up to keep 1,000 rounds per gun actually on the gun position, and in the summer of 1917 the BEF regularly got through a million eighteen-pounder rounds (one nature of ammunition amongst many) every single week, and might fire a million rounds a day at the height of the Passchendaele battle. The impact of ammunition production on the social and economic fabric of Britain lies beyond the compass of this story. But its impact on the ground is a matter of enduring record, as we can still see in the 'artillery landscape' at places like Beaumont Hamel.

Fig. 80 shows Faffémont farm, near Combles on the Somme, on 26 April 1916, well before the pre-battle bombardment. It was then part of the German second position, and the distinctive 'Grecian key' profile of trenches, highlighted by excavated chalk, is very evident. By the time Fig. 81 was taken, on 28 July, the area had been subjected to extensive shelling. The site was still in German hands, but the buildings had been destroyed and the

Fig. 80

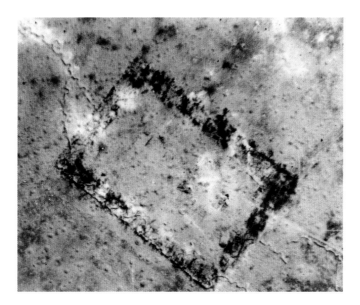

Fig. 81

surrounding trees reduced to matchwood. On 1 September, when Fig. 82 was taken, the site was in the front line – the German front trench runs in a diagonal curl across the image – but was to be taken very shortly. Three members of 1/2nd London Regiment, a Territorial battalion affiliated to the Royal Fusiliers, still lie there in isolated graves.

Fig. 82

Fig. 83

Amongst the papers of Captain C.E. Townley, a wartime-commissioned infantry officer who later served as an intelligence officer with the Royal Flying Corps, is Fig. 83. It shows the British line at Polderhoek, just north of the Menin Road east of Ypres, on 18 March 1918, and marks the high-water mark of British gains in that sector during the third battle of Ypres. He has annotated the photograph, and written on its back: 'I visited this end of March and crossed by [white] dotted line to pillboxes of Jut Farm.' Although the journey cannot have been more than 200 yards each way, it was evidently a trip worth remembering. The photograph gives no real idea of scale, but the letters on it stand about as high as the concrete walls of the pillbox, and are rather lower than the shattered poplar trees that once graced the château's driveway.

Fig. 84

Fig. 85

Photographers naturally tended to photograph shells from a safe distance. Fig. 84, taken by a gunner subaltern, is more unsettling. The high-explosive shell has landed close, but has buried itself in wet soil before exploding, so that much of its mischief has been directed upwards. One description of German fire on 1 July 1916 likened shells falling rapidly in the same spot to 'a thick belt of poplar trees', and we can see why. This shell's target is the horse lines of an artillery battery. Killing the enemy's horses deprived his guns and ammunition wagons of their motive power and, because both sides relied on horses for first-line transport of other supplies, killing them left men hungry and thirsty. Fig. 85 shows a team of gun-mules caught by shellfire on the St-Jean–Ypres road salient. In Fig. 86 the shell has landed very close to the photographer, and the blurred image gives some sense of its blind elemental force.

Fig. 86

Although British accounts dwell on the shocking effects of German *Fig. 87*
artillery fire, one German told his captors on the Somme that they had no *(opposite)*
idea what shellfire was like until they had lived through a British bombardment. Not only did the British build ever more guns and ensure that
they were liberally supplied with ammunition, but increasingly they concentrated their heavy guns into artillery groups under centralised command,
like the 25th Heavy Artillery Group RGA at Ypres in April 1918, with its
twenty-three heavy guns and howitzers, including a fifteen-inch howitzer
and eight twelve-inch guns or howitzers. This group alone could deliver a
greater weight of shell in a single salvo than the whole of the BEF in August
1914. Fig. 87 and Fig. 88 give some idea of the effect of all this. In the first, a
corpse lies in the flooded wreckage of a German bunker, and in the second

Fig. 88

Fig. 89
(previous
pages)

three German dead, already beginning to melt into the violated earth, lie in the ruins of their trench.

It was a gunner's war, and in some theatres – notably the Western Front and Gallipoli – the infantryman lived and died in the shadow of the shell. At Gallipoli the whole Allied position was so exposed that long-range Turkish guns across the straits could fire into its rear: Fig. 89 (*previous pages*) shows a shell from *Asiatic Annie* landing in the sea, just short of the road built along the coast to give a measure of covered resupply. In Palestine and Mesopotamia conditions were different, because there was never the same density of troops to space, or guns to yard of front. Whenever troops paused, though, they dug in, and the war went to earth not only on the Western Front, but in sectors like Gaza, where static defence initially conferred upon the Turks the advantages enjoyed by their German allies in the west.

On the Western Front the first trenches were simple: short, unconnected lines which might shelter a single section of infantry with eight or so men. By

Fig. 90

Fig. 91

the autumn of 1914 the British were forming a continuous front line, digging a support line immediately behind, and beginning to run communication trenches from rear to front so that soldiers could enter and leave front-line trenches without being observed. In that first winter of the war, though, trenches were primitive and uncomfortable, not least because much of the ground held by the British sector was low-lying.

The 11th Hussars were one of the smartest regiments in the army, and Crown Prince Wilhelm of Prussia was their colonel-in-chief. In Fig. 90 we see him at a pre-war polo match, with Major Pitman holding the sticks and Lieutenant Colonel Tyndale Biscoe looking towards the chauffeur of the Prince's car. The regiment took part in the retreat from Mons in August 1914 (Fig. 91), and, fighting dismounted, helped hold Messines Ridge that

Fig. 92

autumn. Among the officers killed was Captain the Hon. Arthur ('Jack') Annesley, son of the 11th Viscount Valentia (Fig. 92). It was an open secret in London society that he had been having an affair with a diplomat's wife, Winifred Bennett, and the commander-in-chief, Field Marshal Sir John French (a 19th Hussar), called on her when on leave in London to offer his condolences, and was himself soon involved in a relationship with her that lasted most of the war.

Lieutenant R.L. Hartman photographed Lieutenant Fritz Renton (Fig. 93) in the relaxed way of the mounted arm, reading the *Tatler* in a wood near Ypres in March 1915. Renton is wearing his service dress cap, two figures in the rear have gorblimey hats, and Sergeant Porter sports a cap-comforter. There is probably little danger, though, for close examination of Sergeant Porter's rifle reveals that it is not cocked. Lieutenant Colonel Pitman was also

Fig. 93
(opposite)

busy with his camera, and Fig. 94 shows the headquarters of the 9th Lancers, a bunker built of sandbags and wood-revetted earth, with signal rockets ready. The two seated figures, captioned as Bimbo Reynolds and Rex Benson, do not look like officers in one of the most up-market regiments on the *Army List*. On the right of the photograph is an abandoned rum-jar, marked 'SRD', for Supply Reserve Depot, though most thought the letters stood for Seldom Reaches Destination.

That winter the first goatskin coats arrived. They came in a variety of colours, but were often unhelpfully light. Although they attracted both moisture and mud, and were notably goaty even when dry, they were very popular in that first chilly winter of trench warfare. Fig. 95 shows a group from 1st Battalion the Rifle Brigade in its finery, with several wonderful Old Bill faces: the corporal sitting second from the right in the front row is *not* amused.

Fig. 94

Fig. 95

In 1915 trenches took on the characteristics that defined them for the rest of the war. A standard fire trench was about seven to eight feet deep, with a sump running along its bottom, covered with wooden duckboards. A parapet of beaten earth crowned the trench on the enemy side, with a similar parados to the rear. A firestep of earth, sandbags or even wood enabled a soldier to step up and look (or shoot) across the parapet. Fig. 96 (*overleaf*) shows a captured German trench at Ovillers on the Somme in July 1916. The original firestep is on the left, but the trench has been 'reversed' by having a new firestep hacked out of what was originally its back. Arriving in an enemy trench without digging tools invited disaster, for until the trench was reversed there was no real way of dealing with a counter-attack.

Fire trenches were never straight but had a series of bays (facing the enemy) and traverses (running at an angle to the bays). This arrangement reduced the effect of a shell bursting squarely in the trench, and made it hard for attackers to fight their way along it. At intervals a 'bomb-stop', usually a barbed-wire gate, was installed to prevent lateral exploitation of a

Fig. 96
(*overleaf*)

break-in. The bomb-stop in Fig. 97 is in the Cambrin sector, and is guarded *Fig. 97*
(opposite) by a sentry of 1/7th Sherwood Foresters, wearing the 1914 pattern leather equipment. Communication trenches running back to the rear had no bays and traverses, whose existence made it hard to lug wounded along a front-line trench, but were rarely absolutely straight. The Royal Irish Rifles lieutenant colonel in Fig. 98 is sloshing, on 7 February 1918, along a communication trench which has been crumbled by winter frost and then turned into a quagmire by the thaw. This sector south of the Somme had been taken over from the French. Some trenches were very poor, and there was insufficient manpower to improve them sufficiently before the Germans attacked on 21 March. The men on the jacket of this book are making their way along a rather better communication trench, though it is easy to see why many sectors had one-way circuits in their communication trenches to prevent traffic jams, for there was often little enough space for two heavily-laden soldiers to pass.

Fig. 98

Fig. 99

Trench warfare helped change the soldier's visual profile: compare the extemporised winter plumage of the Rifle Brigade in Fig. 95 with the soldiers of 12th East Yorkshire, photographed near Arleux in January 1918, in Fig. 99. Both of the latter are wearing sleeveless flannel-lined leather jerkins over their tunics, have their webbing equipment well-fitted over their jerkins, with their respirators in the 'ready' position, and have the working parts of their rifles protected by canvas covers. The sergeant major (we can just make out the crown on his cuff) is ensuring that the rocket fuses are hanging clear for ease of lighting. When the guns supporting his battalion were not engaged on any other task they would be laid on the 'SOS' task, the spot most likely to require artillery fire at short notice, and would be fired if the defenders fired rockets in a pre-arranged sequence, say red over white.

Trench warfare inspired the development of new weapons and the refinement of older ones. The British Army went to war without a hand grenade. In the first year of the war it extemporised, for example by filling empty jam-tins with gun-cotton ignited by a fuse: Fig. 100 shows two Australians preparing jam-tin bombs at Gallipoli. One is chopping up sections of barbed wire to insert into the bomb to increase its fragmentation.

Fig. 100

Both wear felt slippers, for this was no place to strike a spark. The Mills bomb (very similar to the 36 Grenade of Word War II) was a huge improvement in safety, reliability and lethal effect. The soldier in Fig. 101 is preparing Mills bombs. They arrived in boxes of twelve, thickly coated with preservation wax

Fig. 101

Fig. 102

which had to be removed before they could be fused. A Mills bomb could be blasted on its way by a ballestite cartridge from a cup-discharger on a rifle. In contrast, the smaller Hales rifle grenade was connected to a steel rod which fitted into the weapon's barrel. The bored soldier in Fig. 102 is manning a Hales grenade-launcher in a front-line trench on the Salonika front: a grenade box stands open on the left.

The development of grenades, grenade-launchers and trench mortars led to the disappearance of earlier, extemporised weapons of trench warfare like *Fig. 103* the catapult manned by a Naik [Corporal] Lachman of 1/4th Gurkha Rifles *(opposite)* at Gallipoli (Fig. 103). The major breakthrough for the British came in early

1915 when Wilfred Stokes developed his mortar, basically a steel tube resting on a baseplate and supported by a bipod. A bomb was slipped into the muzzle and fired automatically when it hit the fixed firing-pin at the base of the barrel. Fig. 104 shows the three-inch Stokes mortar, the most common mortar in the army: there were 1,600 of them in France at the beginning of 1918, but only 353 in Egypt, Salonika and Mesopotamia at the same time, an index of the primacy of the Western Front and the dominance of trench warfare there. Careful application of a magnifying glass shows that the bomb being inserted into the weapon's muzzle still has its safety pin in place, so this West Yorkshire detachment is simply going through the motions to gratify the photographer. The weapon's 4.5 kg bomb had a maximum range of 1,200 yards. Fig. 105 shows soldiers of the King's Own Yorkshire Light Infantry fusing mortar bombs. In contrast to the previous photograph this is a serious business, and there are no shy smiles for the camera.

Fig. 104 (opposite)

Fig. 105

137

Fig. 106

Both 1.75-inch and two-inch Vickers mortars fired a 'toffee-apple' bomb, so called because its iron spigot fitted down the weapon's barrel, making spigot and projectile look like a huge toffee-apple. Fig. 106 shows a two-inch mortar in a well sandbagged emplacement in Mesopotamia. Its detachment are wearing both neck-covers and spine-pads to mitigate the fierce heat. Granddaddy of them all was the 9.2-inch mortar, its huge projectile known as a 'Flying Pig'. Lieutenant Robert Perry captioned Fig. 107, his 1917 photograph of a 9.2-inch mortar and its officer, 'A Brigade TMB [Trench Mortar Battery] wallah'. From 1916 the two-inch mortar battery attached to each brigade took its brigade's number, and there was a single divisional heavy mortar battery. Trench mortar personnel were infantrymen, sent off by their battalions in response to one of the frequent demands to bring the mortars up to strength, and were often neither the brightest nor the best. It was a dangerous job, for mortars drew counter-battery fire, and an unpopular one too, for soldiers manning a sector resented the fact that mortarmen might arrive, shoot from a suitable sap-head near the front line, and decamp before return fire arrived.

*Fig. 107
(opposite)*

Fig. 108

The army went to war in 1914 with two Vickers machine guns in each infantry battalion and cavalry regiment. Fig. 108 shows a Vickers being fired at night, probably on 'fixed lines' which would enable it to hit known positions. Though I am suspicious about the light required for the photograph, at least the weapon contains a full ammunition belt, and some rounds have evidently been fired from it. There is little doubt about the Vickers in Fig. 109: the photographer has his head well down, and the gun's No. 2 (right) is supporting the loaded belt as it enters the gun's mechanism.

In 1915 these guns were grouped into eight-gun brigade machine-gun companies, and when the Machine Gun Corps was formed that October the officers and men of these companies were rebadged to wear the corps' distinctive crossed-guns emblem. Charles Caddick-Adams had joined 5/North

Fig. 109

Fig. 110

Staffordshire, based at Burton-on-Trent, in 1910. It was very much a band of brothers, for most of the officers had been to Newcastle-under-Lyme High School (where Charles had been a member of the OTC), and the men worked in the potteries. He was his battalion's machine-gun officer on mobilisation: in Fig. 110 he is riding off to war through a Pottery town with his men behind him, their single machine-guns in the cart. Just before the battle of Loos in 1915 he took over all the guns in the brigade because the brigade machine-gun officer was suddenly taken ill.

Caddick-Adams' division, 46th North Midland, was committed to a hopeless attack on 27 September, and 5/North Staffordshire was hard hit. Even before its leading companies could reach the front line, 'all the officers and most of the men had fallen'. Caddick-Adams found that his last-minute posting had spared him, and he never, during the course of a long life, forgot it. Fig. 111 (*overleaf*) shows him commanding 137th Machine-Gun Company (supporting 137th Infantry Brigade) at Amiens in April 1917. When machine-gun companies were combined into battalions in 1918 he became second in command of 46th Machine Gun Battalion, and ended the war a major with a Military Cross.

Fig. 111
(overleaf)

137 Machine

un Company.   '1917'

Amiens.

The centralisation of Vickers guns was made possible by the introduction of the Lewis light machine gun (for the infantry) and the Hotchkiss (for the cavalry). The Lewis, with cooling jacket round its barrel and its forty-seven-round pan magazine, became one the most easily recognised weapons of the war. Despite initial concerns that its arrival could never compensate for the disappearance of the Vickers, it became popular despite its thirty-pound weight, and the Germans used captured weapons on a large scale. By early 1918 an infantry platoon, in theory an officer and thirty-six men, had a Lewis gun section with one gun and nine ammunition-carriers, and by mid-1918 there were at least two guns per platoon. In Fig. 112 we see a Lewis gun team covering the Lys canal at St-Venant during the April 1918 German offensive. The No. 1 has the weapon in the aim, and the fact that its backsight is raised suggests that he is serious about his work. His No. 2 has a box of filled magazines to hand, and holds one ready to pass across when his mate calls for it.

Fig. 113 is a well-known shot of Brigadier General J. Campbell VC addressing 137th Brigade (in which Charles Caddick-Adams served, from start to finish) from the captured bridge over the St-Quentin canal at Riqueval

Fig. 112

Fig. 113 (opposite)

in October 1918, and is a useful counterweight to the misfortunes suffered by these Midlanders at Loos and on the first day of the Somme. It tells us a good deal about the army in the last months of the war. There are lots of youngsters here, and some of the men still wear the lifejackets 'borrowed' from cross-Channel ferries to help with the canal crossing. There are several Lewis guns too: one team just below the centre of the photograph appears to have chalked something on the barrel of their gun. Perhaps it is as well that we cannot quite make out what it is.

As their tactics evolved, infantry grew adept at 'leaning on the barrage' to ensure that they arrived on an enemy position before their opponents had had time to emerge from their dugouts and man their machine guns: by 1917 it was reckoned that attackers should move about fifty yards behind a barrage, even though by doing so they might lose a man or two. The staff *Fig. 114* developed plans which allocated individual objectives to brigades and

Fig. 115

divisions, and then moved fresh formations through these to attack more distant objectives. The advance was preceded by a creeping barrage, and pauses while follow-up units leapfrogged forward were covered by a standing barrage. Although the Arras attack of April 1917 eventually fell short of expectation, its early stages saw a remarkably successful advance. Fig. 114 helps us understand why. This photograph was taken on 9 April, the first day of the battle, and shows infantry 'leapfrogging' in small columns through another battalion which is holding freshly-captured ground. They advanced not in lines, but in the chequerboard blobs of 'artillery formation'.

Brigadier General Roland Boys Bradford VC, the youngest British general of the twentieth century, killed in Bourlon Wood in 1917 at the age of twenty-five, summed up artillery formation as 'a number of small columns at varying intervals and distances, scattered over the front across which we have to advance'. Although the image in Fig. 115 is of poor quality (it was taken by the Rev. Basil Bond, chaplain to 1/5th Essex), it shows infantry at the first battle of Gaza waiting to go forward in the clumps which would open out into artillery formation when the advance began.

The tank made its first appearance on the Somme in September 1916: *Fig. 116 (opposite top)* forty-nine were used, of which eighteen actually saw action. The Mark 1 tank that fought on the Somme (Fig. 116) came in two varieties. The male had two *Fig. 117 (opposite bottom)* six-pounder naval guns and four machine guns, while the female had six machine guns. Both types were manned by a commander and a crew of seven, initially part of the Heavy Branch, Machine Gun Corps, which became the Tank Corps in 1917. They were painfully slow, capable of just 3.7 mph on flat ground. At first, although German artillery could destroy them with direct hits, the sheer shock of their appearance demoralised the defence, and more were rendered inoperable by the ground or breakdown than by enemy fire. The Germans soon developed an anti-tank rifle (a captured weapon is proudly shown off by New Zealand gunner officers in Fig. 117) simply by scaling up the bolt-action infantry rifle for a 13.2mm round. Tanks played little useful part in the third battle of Ypres, largely because the ground was unsuitable. Robert Perry, sheltering in the lee of a damaged German pillbox, photographed a 'tank arriving to assist a bogged comrade' (Fig. 118). There

Fig. 118

Fig. 119

was no help for most mired tanks, and the area between Hooge Ridge and Hellfire Corner on the Menin road became, as Fig. 119 shows, a veritable tanks' graveyard.

By November 1917, when tanks were used on a much larger scale at Cambrai, with 476 machines involved, they had been improved, but German gunners had by that time been taught how to take them on with direct fire.

Fig. 120

Moreover, the Germans were now digging unusually wide trenches in an effort to stop tanks. In Fig. 120 we see how *Hyacinth*, a Mark IV tank of H Battalion, Tank Corps, has failed to negotiate a second-line trench just west of Ribecourt on the Cambrai battlefield. Perhaps more remarkable than the stalled breakthrough at Cambrai, where British gains were largely swallowed up in a well-handled counter-attack, was the Amiens battle of 8 August 1918, when tanks helped bring about a substantial German defeat.

Although they made a promising start in the autumn of 1914, armoured cars were too lightly protected to be much use on the Western Front. They came into their own in other theatres, especially in the Arabian peninsula, where Rolls-Royce armoured cars, based on the Silver Ghost, provided valuable support for the Arab revolt. In Fig.121, a photograph taken by Captain Raymond Goslett, we see Talbot armoured cars and Ford tenders on their way to Abu Lassal, probably in early 1918, from T.E. Lawrence's collection in the Imperial War Museum.

Fig. 121

Fig. 122

Tanks and armoured cars were, in their different ways, taking on roles once carried out by the cavalry, with the heavy tank accomplishing breakthrough and the whippet undertaking pursuit. Few subjects have generated more ill-informed comment than that of cavalry on the Western Front. They were not over-represented in the British Army in 1914, and

Fig. 123

neither (although successive commanders-in-chief, French till December 1915 and Haig thereafter, were cavalrymen) were cavalry officers disproportionately numerous in the chain of command. Haig was probably wrong to keep his cavalry in a single corps, hoping that they would eventually be able to exploit a breakthrough. It is now evident that speed was the key to the exploitation of tactical success, and that a few cavalry closer to the front were more likely to be successful than numerous cavalry further back. Some of the problems confronting cavalry in trench warfare were overcome. Fig. 122 shows men of a Canadian regiment, the Fort Gary Horse, using a trench bridge which they had designed, and with which they provided trench-crossing facilities to the entire cavalry corps.

There were times, even on the Western Front, when cavalry operated very effectively. However, speed was always of the essence. By the time they were injected into the April 1917 Arras attack (Fig. 123 shows them going forward on the tenth) it was already too late, for the German defence had solidified. Dismounted cavalry fought bravely to hold the key village of Monchy le Preux, but German artillery fire butchered their led horses (Fig. 124). Although communication difficulties made it difficult for the cavalry to reach *Fig. 124*

Fig. 125   the front in time to exploit initial success at Cambrai in 1917, the Canadian Cavalry Brigade captured 400 men and nearly 100 machine guns. Lieutenant Harcus Strachan earned the Victoria Cross commanding a squadron of Fort Gary Horse behind German lines that day. Fig. 125 shows Strachan (centre right, with cap and jerkin) at the head of his squadron.

Mounted cavalry were no use at Gallipoli, though a dismounted Yeomanry Division fought there with self-sacrificing bravery. They were valuable in Mesopotamia, and essential in Palestine. In early 1917 the British launched two frontal assaults on Turkish positions blocking the direct route up the Palestine coast at Gaza. It was only in October that Allenby, appointed commander-in-chief in Egypt earlier that year, hooked right round the Turkish flank to Beersheba, thereby unhinging the defence. The attack was spearheaded by the 4th Australian Light Horse Brigade. Trained, like their comrades in the New Zealand Mounted Rifles, to fight on foot and consequently not equipped with swords, the Light Horsemen nevertheless carried out a highly successful mounted charge. Fig. 126 is one of the most controversial photographs of the war. Grave doubts have been raised as to its authenticity, not least because the assertion that a Turk had paused to take the photograph when he might have had other preoccupations seems palpably absurd. However, the commander of 4th ALH Brigade certainly thought it was genuine, and Rex Elliott, a former range-finder with brigade head-quarters, who had been well forward to prepare range charts, testified that he looked back towards the brigade's position and

> saw horsemen in extended order coming over the crest of the ridge . . . as the front line drew nearer I saw that their bayonets were drawn and they were approaching at a hard gallop, having a camera in my haversack I got it out and took a shot, got on my horse and went as fast as I could further out to a flank . . .

If historians continue to bicker over the role of the cavalry, there can be no doubting the importance of engineers: by the end of the war they numbered a quarter of a million officers and men, more than double the size of the entire British regular army as I write. Many of their tasks were wholly traditional. In static defence or the advance they made it easier for their friends to live and to move, and in withdrawal they made life harder for the enemy by destroying bridges and railways and damaging roads. It is wholly fitting that one of the first VCs of the war was won by Captain Theodore Wright RE for demolishing a bridge under heavy fire near Mons on 23 August 1914. He was killed at Vailly on 14 September the same year, shepherding advancing troops across a pontoon bridge over the Aisne. Throughout the war the engineers *Fig. 126*

Fig. 127 (previous pages) bridged a variety of water obstacles, from the stately rivers of northern France to the Tigris and Euphrates. In Fig. 127 (*previous pages*) infantry are about to cross an engineer-manned pontoon bridge thrown across the Somme at Peronne to replace a bridge blown up by the Germans on their retreat to the Hindenburg Line in 1917. Engineers were paid significantly better than the infantry, which caused a good deal of friction, but there were times when they unquestionably earned their money. Bridges were attractive targets, and while most troops could cross them quickly engineers were compelled to remain in situ to maintain and repair them.

Royal Engineers were also responsible for the construction and maintenance of railways, and for manning both engines and vessels used for inland water transport. In Fig. 128 we see engineers building a light railway, while Fig. 129 shows a busy loco yard behind the lines, possibly at Hazebrouck, the main British railhead in northern France. The engineers tried to enlist men with relevant trades (indeed, the fact that many of their private soldiers and NCOs were skilled tradesmen was held to justify their *Fig. 128* higher pay), and many of the soldiers in this photograph would have been

Fig. 129

pre-war railwaymen. It emphasises the fact that the burgeoning world of the rear ate up growing quantities of men and, increasingly, women too, who were uniformed and disciplined, but had little in common with those essential pawns of warfare in the infantry.

Engineers had long been responsible for subterranean mines, and had added submarine mines to their repertoire in 1871. Mining on the Western Front grew to assume the proportions of a major industry. The Germans were first in the field, exploding mines beneath the Indian Corps' sector at Festubert. Thanks largely to the efforts of John Norton Griffiths, Conservative MP, civil engineer and temporary RE officer, the British began to form tunnelling companies in early 1915, and they exploded their first mine, under Hill 60 at Ypres, that April. Thereafter, although the Germans always fought back, exploding mines of their own beneath British trenches and sometimes blowing in the tunnels that were being driven underneath their own defences, the British steadily gained the upper hand, and mines played a major role in the British attacks on the Somme in 1916 and at Messines Ridge the following year.

Perhaps the best-known photograph of a mine going up was taken at 7.20 on the morning of 1 July 1916 by Ernest Brooks from a position very close

Fig. 130

to White City, between Auchonvillers and Beaumont Hamel (Fig. 130). This was exploded beneath Hawthorn Ridge redoubt, and although the redoubt was destroyed the attackers lost the race for the crater. Fig. 131 shows a miner at work on the approach tunnel to this same mine-chamber, hacking his way through Somme chalk, which was a good deal more forgiving than the complex geology of the Ypres salient. Sometimes the Germans broke into British workings, and often they used small mines, called camouflets, to blow in tunnels. In Fig. 132 two miners have stopped work while an officer listens for sounds of hostile digging.

Fig. 131

Fig. 132

Not all mines exploded, often because the circuitry connecting the exploder to the detonators had been damaged by damp or by enemy action. Large mines were devastating: the Spanbroekmolen mine, one of the nineteen exploded beneath Messines Ridge, contained 91,000 pounds of ammonal, and had taken 171 Tunnelling Company Royal Engineers a year to dig. Pillboxes nearby were overturned, as can be seen in Fig. 133: some defenders were simply vaporised, others were blown high into the air or buried in their dugouts, and some were slain without visible sign by the effect of the blast on their lungs.

Fig. 133

Fig. 134

Photograph reproduced with the kind permission of the Royal Engineers Museum and Library

One VC was awarded to a tunneller. William Hackett of Mexborough (Fig. 134) was a miner from Manvers Main Colliery, with twenty-three years' experience underground, who had tried to join the infantry four times, but was rejected because of his age: a father of two, he was then forty-two years old. The engineers were happy to take him on, and on 23 June 1916 he was at work in the Shaftesbury shaft near Red Dragon Crater in the Givenchy sector. The Germans blew in the tunnel, cutting off five miners. After working for twenty-four hours they had made an opening large enough to escape through, and a rescue party on the other side of the earth-fall pulled three to safety. Hackett helped the men through the hole and could easily have followed, but would not budge until his chum Thomas Collins, a Welsh miner wounded by the explosion, had been taken to safety. He told the rescuers: 'I am a tunneller. I must look after the others first.' He could see that the hole was getting smaller by the minute, and knew the danger of sliding earth. The gallery soon fell in, and although the rescuers dug for four days they could not find him. His daughter presented the VC to the Royal Engineers museum in 1966, remarking: 'It seems such a little thing to exchange for his life.' But this was a generation to which little things mattered a great deal.

4

Life and Death

Gallipoli was arguably the most hazardous of all the war's theatres, because everyone on the peninsula, regardless of rank or occupation, was vulnerable to artillery. Some positions, like Quinn's Post in the ANZAC sector, were especially dangerous. Fig. 135, a fine photograph taken by the Australian official historian, Charles Bean, shows men of 4th Australian Infantry Brigade just behind the post after it was retaken on 29 May 1915. In spots like *Fig. 135*

Fig. 136

this the enemy was scarcely ever out of grenade range, snipers were a constant problem, and shrapnel burst overhead, with empty shrapnel shells spinning off into the gully behind, looking, as one British machine-gun officer wrote, like tumbler pigeons.

Although the setting could be majestic, inducing classically-educated young officers to muse on Homer's wine-dark sea or to beg for aid from flame-capped Achilles, the climate was savage, and 1/3rd London was all but destroyed by a flash flood in the autumn of 1915. Fig. 136 shows four of the battalion's officers (the CO second from the right) in an improvised shelter in its aftermath. In contrast, pitched battle was relatively rare in East Africa, but disease was a killer. There, only 376 officers and men were killed in action, but over 42,000 died of sickness.

This war, like most others, alternated terror with boredom and combat with drudgery. Even for an infantryman on the Western Front time spent in front-line trenches was outstripped by periods further back by a proportion of three or four to one. An infantry battalion would alternate tours of trench duty (going 'up the line') with periods in reserve, at rest or training for coming operations. Units bound for the front marched out from their camp or billets in full martial panoply, often accompanied part of the way by their bands. As it approached the front a battalion would change from column of fours into a more dispersed formation, perhaps 'staggered file', on both sides of the road, and would eventually fall into single file (always frustrating and prone to sudden breaks or lengthy waits) for the last leg. The advancing companies, trudging forward, would be met by guides (we see some waiting north-east of Trones Wood on the Somme in

Fig. 137

September 1916 in Fig. 137) who would take them up to the sector they were to hold, where they would find the outgoing unit deeply anxious to move.

The pattern of life in the trenches centred on stand-to on either side of dawn and dusk, in theory because this was a time when attack was likely, but in practice because it enabled commanders at all levels to assert control and sense the pulse of their commands. Fig. 138, depicting men of a Lancashire

Fig. 138

Fusilier battalion near Messines in 1916, may well show the scene before evening stand-to. Some men are already standing up in the trench, and one has his bayonet ready: fixing bayonets was a standard stand-to precaution. In the centre, Lewis gunners are assembling their weapon after cleaning it, and their platoon commander (wearing a single star on his soldier's greatcoat, for the putty-coloured officer's British Warm was lethal in a front-line trench) is seeing how the task is going. There is a gas-warning hooter, powered by compressed air, near the gunners, and up to the right is a wind vane which showed when an easterly wind made German use of gas more likely.

On a normal day in the trenches very little happened, although there might always be casualties caused by snipers or desultory shelling. Men napped on the firestep or in 'funk-holes' chipped out of the forward wall of the trench, though the practice of making these cubby-holes was repeatedly forbidden because they weakened the trench's structure. Officers – and the more fortunate amongst the men – would spend much of their time in dugouts. The best were those captured from the Germans, who, generally content to sit on the defensive in the west, built some luxurious specimens. *Fig. 139* Fig. 139, a photograph taken by Ernest Brooks in November 1916, shows

Fig. 140

officers of the Queen's Royal Surrey Regiment in a captured dugout, complete with panelling and wallpaper. The subaltern on the left is reading the label of an HMV record, and the *Daily Mirror* does duty as an extra lampshade. The helmeted figure on the right is the war correspondent Basil Clark. The setting is strangely similar to the set of R.C. Sherriff's play *Journey's End*, and Sherriff (initially turned down for a commission because he had not been to public school) eventually became an officer in the East Surreys, known to officers of the Queen's as 'the other Surrey regiment'.

Many German pillboxes were indestructible save by direct hits from heavy guns, though repeated near-misses sometimes caused them to slide into the surrounding crater-fields, suffocating their occupants. Fig. 140 shows a pillbox in the Ypres salient, badly battered by several hits but still usable. Piled against its base are tins. Front-line water was rarely much improved by the fact that it was carried in the same five-gallon cans used to bring petrol (to power generators) to the line. Although these were meant to be 'flamed out' after containing fuel, the water that emerged from them was normally tainted: front-line tea had a unique tang of petrol and condensed milk. The interior of such a pillbox would resemble the one in Fig. 141 (*overleaf*), where men of the West Yorkshire Regiment wait in late

Fig. 141 (overleaf)

Fig. 142   September or early October 1917 during Third Ypres. The lance corporal on the left is tucking into a tin of bully beef, and his mate in the left centre has a large chunk of bread. No photograph can catch the smell of earth, decay, high explosive, latrines (human waste overlaid with chloride of lime), the half-buried dead, fried bacon and unwashed humanity. This was a pre-deodorant age, and a man might very well not change his shirt and under-wear for a week.

It was not until a soldier came out of the line that he could begin to restore his dignity. Fig. 142 shows three members of the 4th South African Infantry (South African Scottish). There was a South African brigade in 9th (Scottish) Division, and its defence of Delville Wood on the Somme in July 1916 left an enduring mark on history: of 3,155 all ranks, only eighteen officers and 702 men emerged unscathed. This trio is making the most of some summer sunshine in Carnoy Valley, just behind the line.

In some sectors (though not in all units) men were expected to shave every day. Fig. 143 shows Lieutenant Colonel Philip 'Blobs' Robertson of the Cameronians, with his adjutant, Captain H.H. Lee, in the background, shaving during the retreat from Mons in 1914, in a photograph taken by Lieutenant Money. Robertson was an officer of the old school, and would have regarded it as unthinkable to appear unshaven. He went on to command 19th Infantry Brigade, and in July 1915, on a visit to the trenches, complained to the CO of 2/Royal Welch Fusiliers that his battalion had not yet submitted a formal defence scheme. The nettled CO wrote on the back of a used envelope: 'I will hold my line to the last. If the enemy penetrates he will be driven out. If the troops to right or left give way I will form a flank.' Robertson was promoted to command 17th (Northern) Division in July 1916, and made a very good job of it, going round his trenches four mornings a week. In 1917 he was one of the three divisional commanders who protested directly to Haig about Allenby's conduct of the Arras battle, taking a huge risk with his career. But Haig backed him, and he retired a (well-shaven) knight.

Fig. 143

A contrast is provided by the men in Fig. 144, shaving near Beaumont Hamel on the Somme in November 1916. Both have classic old-soldier haircuts and moustaches. At least in theory it had been forbidden to shave the upper lip until that summer. Not all obeyed the rule (the commander of the Canadian Corps, Sir Arthur Currie, was notably unmoustachioed), but it was only after an officer had been court-martialled for shaving that the adjutant general in France, Sir Nevil Macready, got the rule (a reflection of the days when facial hair betokened martial virility) changed. Younger soldiers often sported a haircut which blitzed back and sides but left a long lock at the front, which could be tugged out of an edged-backwards steel helmet to show a little individuality while breaking none of the rules.

Although it was possible to do some work, like the omnipresent sandbag-filling, shown in Fig. 145 (this is a communication trench, for there is no firestep), in the daylight, the front really came to life after dark. Battalions in the line repaired their trenches and the barbed wire in their front, protecting their wiring parties with standing patrols on the German side of the British wire. Carrying parties would be sent back to collect 'trench stores', things like barbed wire, wire pickets, duckboards and empty sandbags, and carry them up to the front line. In Fig. 146 we see an unusual shot of troops carrying duckboards near Cambrai: they are able to go 'over the top' rather than use a

Fig. 144 (opposite top)

Fig. 145 (opposite bottom)

Fig. 146

Fig. 147 communication trench because of the cover of darkness. The night sky is laced by illuminants, which included everything from the simple rise-and-fall flares of Verey pistols to 'star-shells', parachute-illuminating rounds fired by artillery. Wire entanglements in front of reserve positions could be constructed in daylight. Fig. 147 shows Highlanders converting a roll of barbed wire into a concertina by wrapping it round a frame made from angle-iron pickets. The finished concertina would be turned on its side and pulled out, to be anchored with pickets at regular intervals. There are no wiring-gloves in evidence, through the soldier to the left front seems to be trying to protect his hands with straw.

Soldiers in the line would generally receive one hot meal a day, often taken forward to them after last light. It was cooked, under the quartermaster's supervision, by the battalion's cooks, using wheeled field cookers. Fig. 148 shows a lugubrious group of Hampshires in the first winter of the war, with the men on the right holding 'Dixies', the multi-purpose cooking vessel. Cooked food went forward in hay-boxes, and was doled out into men's mess-tins.

Fig. 148

Fig. 149 shows Lancashire Fusiliers having food ladled from a Dixie. Wise quartermasters ensured that troops received simple rib-sticking grub that could be eaten one-handed with a spoon: soldiers sometimes carried a spoon tucked into the top of a puttee. All-in stew was popular, as were porridge and pea soup. Troops in the line made their own brew-ups with a variety of individual burners, known as Tommy cookers, ranging from spirit stoves to tins fuelled

Fig. 149

by rifle oil and flannelette. They used officially-supplied rations (Maconochie's meat and vegetable stew and corned beef chief amongst them) and their own provisions, either purchased when the battalion was out of the line or sent from home by family and friends, to cook something at lunchtime. In parts of the line it was possible to cook breakfast, with bacon carried up the night before, tasting, like most fresh food that appeared at the front, of the sandbags used to transport it. *Fig. 150 (opposite top)*

Fig. 151 (opposite bottom)

In Fig. 150 a group of soldiers celebrate Christmas 1916 on the Somme in the bleak but protective surroundings of a shell-hole, their appetite for cake apparently undiminished by the proximity of a grave. Fig. 151 shows the distribution of rations out of the line, with bread, tinned jam and tinned sardines being divided up (under the supervision of the company quartermaster sergeant, standing on the left) into shares which ration orderlies would take back, slung in a groundsheet, to their sections. The fourth soldier from the right is wearing an identity bracelet, and the right-hand man's sleeve bears a patch which would help cognoscenti to deduce his division and brigade. The standard army loaf weighed two pounds: one loaf between three men was a fair issue, and six to a loaf was tight. Fig. 152 shows an army bakery hard at work producing ration

Fig. 152

Fig. 153

loaves. Troops were also supplied with biscuits which, then as now, were hard and unforgiving, not least to a generation with poor teeth: iron rations indeed.

Out of the line, men often lived in camps composed of tents, or one of the war's most notable inventions, Nissen huts, named for their inventor, the then Major Peter Nissen, a Canadian mining engineer. Based on corrugated steel, they could be erected without the need for specialist labour, and formed the basis for the US Army's Quonset hut. Fig. 153 shows a hutted camp on the

Fig. 154

old Somme battlefield after the German withdrawal to the Hindenburg Line, further east, in the spring of 1917. There were quirkier quarters: Fig. 154 shows men climbing into a disused water tower near Arras. Troops were often billeted on civilian inhabitants. French local authorities (usually in the person of the commune's mayor, who enjoyed much greater executive authority than his counterpart in Britain) issued billeting orders to citizens. Units used their attached French officers and NCO interpreters (this was where the photographer and artist Paul Maze came into his own) to match weary men to sombre rooms. Some soldiers were pleased enough to slip back into the sorts of communities they might so easily have sprung from. In Fig. 155 a soldier with three long-service chevrons and a single wound-stripe on his cuff dandles an infant on his knee outside his billet at Adinkerke near *Fig. 155*

Fig. 156   Dunkirk in August 1917: he is showing the child a photograph, presumably of his own family. In Fig. 156 two soldiers have taken benevolent charge of a female refugee, pushing her pram and carrying her luggage.

It was an age when few houses had telephones, and soldiers maintained contact with home through letters and parcels. This worked very efficiently on the Western Front, where there were Base Post Offices at Le Havre and Boulogne (Fig. 157), where post was sorted into battalion bags and sent forward. Generally a letter reached its addressee two days after it was posted in Britain. Things were more difficult on other fronts – for instance, submarine attacks on shipping in the Mediterranean meant that whole consignments of 2,000–3,000 bags destined for Salonika were often lost at sea. Nevertheless, the army's postal services (a branch of the Royal Engineers) coped remarkably well.

All British Expeditionary Forces had a base area close to the main port *Fig. 157* of entry into the theatre. In France, the whole area around the town of Étaples ('Eat Apples', in soldier's slang) on the estuary of the River Canche near Le Touquet became the army's main base. Individuals returning to the front after being wounded, and reinforcements posted to France in small groups ('drafts'), normally landed at Le Havre and went to Étaples, where they carried out continuation or refresher training before being formed into new drafts, often changing their regimental identity in the process, for the journey to the front. Like most transit camps, Étaples was not a popular place. Bonds linking officers, NCOs and men there were weak, and it is no surprise that the only serious mutiny in France occurred there in 1917.

Fig. 158

Most photographs of Étaples show troops drilling or bayonet-training on the sands, but in Fig. 158 we see them being taught target indication. The soldiers come from a variety of arms, and there are some NCOs amongst them, who would doubtless have taught the same subject to their own men. However, it was easy, in the prevailing conditions of trench warfare, for men to become so preoccupied with grenades that they forgot how to use their rifles properly, and as it grew increasingly clear during the Somme battle that the musketry on which the old army had prided itself was a thing of the past, the Étaples syllabus was changed in an effort to improve marksmanship skills. There were also a variety of training schools for officers, NCOs and specialists in the rear areas. At their best these helped raise standards and disseminate best practice, and at worst they gave tired leaders a break from their responsibilities.

Soldiers on the Western Front received occasional home leave, calculated on a battalion roster, and liable to sudden cancellation if a 'show' was scheduled. In the average unit a man might get home for a week a year, but it was undoubtedly easier for the senior and the well-placed to insist on regular leave. Blobs Robertson, with a numerous and much-loved family, got home every three months when a divisional commander. Men with a leave ticket went to Boulogne, usually by train, and were ferried to Folkestone, where they caught the train to Victoria (Fig. 159, *overleaf*). They were expected to *Fig. 159 (overleaf)* wear uniform during leave, and often found picking up the fag-ends of their old lives painful and unsatisfactory. It was hard to tell those you loved most what France was really like, and even harder to relax knowing that your closest friends were still at risk. For some, leave was glimpsed darkly through a blur of drink and sex. For others it was laced with the ineluctable poignancy of love rekindled, and new life glimpsed or created. For all, though, the shadow of Victoria Station and the leave boat was like a death's head at the feast. Fig. 160, with soldiers getting off the boat at Boulogne on 30 January 1918, speaks volumes. The Highlander at the foot of the gangway has four wound-stripes on his cuff, and a face set firm to cope with whatever the future has in store. With the great German offensive brewing there were few worse times to be an infantryman, and I pray that he lived to see his blue hills again.

Units out of the line dealt with a good deal of routine housekeeping. Uniforms had to be deloused and men kept clean, either in bath houses close to the front (former breweries, with their vats and piping, formed an ideal basis for these steamy establishments) or in the sea. Battalions had a small team of tailors under a sergeant, and these were always busy promoting the

Fig. 160

Fig. 161

lucky, demoting the unfortunate, and stitching the burgeoning iconography of patches onto the uniforms of those who came up from Étaples without them. Highland units wore the kilt throughout the war, covered, from 1915, with a khaki apron to protect it and make brighter tartans less visible. Although underwear did not, traditionally, lurk beneath the kilt, in unforgiving climates Scottish soldiers might either cut the legs off army-issue longjohns or avail themselves of 'drawers, anti-gas' issued because gas tended to gravitate towards the warmer parts of the anatomy. Fig. 161 shows the tailors of 5/Seaforth Highlanders sewing on NCOs' chevrons. Units also had their own boot repairers, and there were boot-recycling workshops in the base area, where boots recovered from casualties were checked and repaired, as we see in Fig. 162, before reissue.

Even if units were in theory at rest, work was rarely far away, and the bane of life for the infantry in all theatres of war was the need to provide working parties for all sorts of tasks that demanded raw muscle, which led to constant

Fig. 162

tension between the chain of command and infantry officers who feared that their men were worked so heavily that they risked becoming exhausted (and no better-trained) while out of the line. Fig. 163 shows a carrying party, this time moving chimneys for stoves near Pozières on the old Somme battlefield

Fig. 163

in February 1917. In 1915 each division was given a pioneer battalion, badged as infantry and capable of bearing a hand in the line if the situation demanded it, but generally employed on labouring duties in the divisional area. Further down the scale came purpose-raised labour battalions, with a tiny complement of officers, raised from men unfit for full service. In Fig. 164 we see men of 12/Black Watch, raised as a labour battalion at Blairgowrie in 1916, widening a road on the Somme in November of that year: headquarters 4th Division is up the steps on the right. In 1917, as part of the periodic rejigging of the structure of labour units, the battalion was transferred en bloc to the Labour Corps, which had 100,000 men in France alone by the middle of that year, and almost 400,000 men on its strength by January 1919.

Fig. 164

Indigenous labour was widely used in most theatres, and on the Western Front, where it was not so easily available, there were South African, Indian, Egyptian, Fijian and Chinese labourers, on a variety of terms of service. Ninety-six thousand Chinese worked for the British in France by early 1918, serving on contracts but subject to military law. Ten of them were shot for killing civilians or fellow Chinese, forming a high proportion of the thirty-nine executions for murder in the army during the war. This figure does not include several 'fatal incidents' involving native workers, including one in which a number of 'escaped' Chinese labourers were shot out of hand. The Chinese labourers in Fig. 165 are working in a sawmill. Trench warfare had an insatiable appetite for timber, and both British pioneer battalions and indigenous labour units were often employed felling trees, preparing and hauling timber.

The great majority of horses and mules in all theatres of war – and the army had 791,696 animals on its strength in 1918 – were used to haul guns or

Fig. 165

wagons. There were only 186,543 riding horses in this total, and these included mounts for horse and field gunners, mounted officers and the cavalry. They required constant attention whether or not a unit was in the line. In Fig. 166, soldiers of the Army Service Corps wearing trench-waders begin the daunting task of removing mud from a mule. Fig. 167 shows troopers of the Royal Scots Greys watering their horses behind the lines in May 1918. In 1914, in an effort to make them less visible, the Greys dyed their horses with Condy's fluid, which often gave them an oddly pink hue, but once it had worn off surviving greys soldiered on undyed.

Fig. 166 (opposite top)

Fig. 167 (opposite bottom)

Dogs were enormously popular. Fig. 168 shows a military policeman fielding some of the terriers who had scampered, in the irrepressible way of their tribe, to join their masters during a Guards Division parade at Lumbres in 1916. There were two branches of the military police, the Military Mounted Police and the Military Foot Police, and this corporal, with his

Fig. 168

Fig. 169

boots and breeches, is a member of the latter. He is not amused. In contrast, the dogs in Fig. 169 are listening to the gramophone with their masters, officers of the Heavy Branch, Machine Gun Corps, at Poperinghe, just behind the Ypres salient, in the summer of 1917. The lieutenant centre right is a member of the corps, and the seated officer on the left is simply attached to it, for he wears the collar-dogs of his own regiment. The white tank emblem on the sleeves of most officers in the photograph shows that they are tank crew, so the photograph must just predate 27 July 1917, when the Tank Corps was formed.

Fig. 170 (opposite top)

Fig. 171 (opposite bottom)

The hounds with Lieutenant Ramsden of the 5th Lancers (Fig. 170), their photograph taken by Paul Maze, are altogether more serious creatures. Some cavalry regiments brought hounds out to France in late 1914, and there was some hunting, to the irritation of the civil authorities, who mumbled unhelpfully about *'chasse gardée'*. Eventually a brigadier general broke his pelvis and the chase was banned by GHQ. One siege battery RGA had a pet cat, seen in Fig. 171 being befriended by the battery commander on the breech of a mighty twelve-inch howitzer. The war's most unusual pet may have been

Fig. 172

Jackie the baboon, mascot of 3rd South African Infantry, who lives on in a photograph (Fig. 172) showing him at lunch. This friendly creature, who always saluted officers, was twice wounded (rising from his pillow to put paw gravely to forehead when the doctor appeared) but survived the war.

Even an infantry division had some 6,000 horses, and horse shows were organised when divisions were out of the line. They included not only turnout competitions, flat races and steeplechases (Lieutenant Colonel Rowland Feilding was to command two infantry battalions, but received his most serious injury when his horse fell at a fence), but also displays by the massed bands of the division. On mobilisation the musicians of regimental bands were assimilated within their units as stretcher-bearers or combatant soldiers: Corporal Edward Thomas, the first British soldier to fire his rifle at the Germans, on 22 August 1914, had been a bandsman. Members of a battalion's corps of drums, a different category of soldier altogether, retained their musical function. In practice some regiments reconstituted their bands to serenade soldiers out of the line or play them into and out of camp. Massed corps of drums could put on a spectacular display. When the first-rate 9th Scottish Division held its horse show at Liencourt near Arras on 13 May 1917 there were 323 pipers and drummers on parade (Fig. 173). The division had fought hard in the Arras offensive only the previous month. Wise *Fig. 173*

Fig. 174

commanders recognised that post-battle reconstitution required careful attention to reinforcing a division's sense of identity, all the more so because, by this stage in the war, men were sent up from Étaples with little regard for their previous regimental affiliations.

Football was commonly played behind the lines, and James Jack, a strait-laced Cameronian, maintained that soldiers always complained that they were tired and then spent all available spare time kicking a ball about. Fig. 174 shows the

Fig. 175

48th Division Cup Final, played between 1/7th Worcesters and 1/7th Warwicks at Trissino in northern Italy in 1918. Sports days were popular, and in Fig. 175 we see 7/Black Watch at leisure at Bailleul aux Cornailles on 10 May 1917. And there was always fishing, enormously popular even though most keen fishermen had to

Fig. 176

rely on improvised tackle: the soldiers in Fig. 176 are keeping their bait in an empty plum-jam tin, the very container that would have been packed with gun-cotton and chopped barbed wire earlier in the war.

Just as horse shows, band concerts and football matches mirrored familiar civilian entertainment, so concert parties were the army's take on the music hall. On the Western Front most divisions and some rear-area commands maintained their own concert parties. Fig. 177 shows the Diamond Troup, the 29th Division's concert party, wearing the popular pierrot costume. Their

Fig. 177

Fig. 178

female lead is a good deal more convincing than the RFC's Kite and Balloon Section's Cinderella in Fig. 178, though the private in the Sherwood Foresters seems delighted to have met a real lady at last. Occasionally female impersonators became unsettlingly persuasive. One subaltern reported a queue of mistaken young officers with chocolates at the stage door, while a seasoned quartermaster, looking at the line-up at a concert party, opined that it had gone too far. There would be 'more stiff pricks than runny noses' in *that* audience.

Drink and sex, those recurrent preoccupations of soldiers across history, always exercised Tommy, but tend not to find their way into albums, official or unofficial. There were increasing numbers of women in the rear areas, many of them drivers, like those we have seen in an earlier chapter. Nurses, whether members of the Queen Alexandra's Nursing Service, Voluntary Aid Detachments, or other volunteer organisations like the Scottish Women's Hospital, were told of the need 'to set an example of discipline and perfect steadiness of character, but also to maintain the most courteous relations with those you are helping in this great struggle'. Fig. 179 shows VAD ambulance drivers at Étaples in June 1917, their vehicle provided by the owners and workforce of the Royal Forest of Dean coalfield.

For every nurse who fell in love with one of her patients, there were dozens more who helped men face pain, disablement and death. They also made their own gentle contribution to the way men treated women. One VAD asked a wounded soldier whether she should begin the letter she was writing for him with 'My dear wife'. 'That sounds fine,' he answered, 'but she'll be wondering I never said that before.' There can be no doubting the burden sustained by nurses. Vera Brittain, herself a VAD, who lost both a brother and a fiancé in the war, wrote movingly of 'dishevelled beds, the stretchers on the floor, the scattered boots and piles of muddy clothing, the brown blankets turned back from smashed limbs bound to splints by filthy *Fig. 179*

Fig. 180

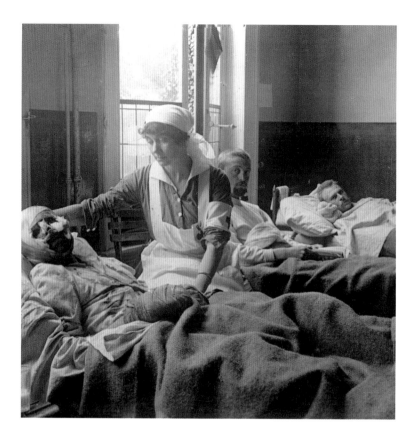

bloodstained bandages'. Fig. 180 would never have appeared in the British press during the war. It was taken in a Belgian hospital by an American photographer, and shows a nurse tending a soldier with appalling facial wounds.

The soldier who found himself tended by one of these 'roses of no man's land' had begun his journey to a warm bed and clean sheets by way of his Regimental Aid Post. Battalion-sized units had their own medical officer, usually a lieutenant or captain in the Royal Army Medical Corps, who acted as his unit's GP when it was out of the line. In it, assisted by a sergeant, orderlies and stretcher-bearers, he presided over the RAP, usually in a forward trench, though not generally in the front line itself. There, in the shelter of a bay, often partly roofed in corrugated 'elephant iron', he carried out a swift assessment of men brought to him by the stretcher-bearers or who staggered there under their own steam. Some were beyond human help, and would simply be given morphine to alleviate their pain. Others would get

Fig. 181

quick life-saving treatment and then be sent back by stretcher to an Advanced Dressing Station, while those whose wounds could wait would follow when there were bearers available.

Walking wounded who could not be dealt with at the RAP made their own way, often helped by prisoners also on their way back, to a Walking Wounded Collecting Station. In Fig. 181 we see Canadian wounded coming back from Third Ypres pausing for a smoke on their way: some kindly soul has given a cigarette to the prisoner. The Scots troops in Fig. 182, on the road

Fig. 182

Fig. 183

near 43rd Casualty Clearing Station at Frévent in April 1918, are aware that they have drawn a good number in war's lottery. Some have the diagnostic label attached to them in their RAP prominently displayed.

Good stretcher-bearers, and there were many, were pearls beyond price. The best were fearless. One man, hard hit in an advance in the last weeks of the war, gratefully reported that the bearers ran up to help as soon as he cried out, and although they were deliberately machine-gunned on the carry back, they stuck to their task like Trojans. The most decorated non-commissioned soldier in the army was a stretcher-bearer, Lance Corporal Bill Coltman of 1/6th North Staffordshire (Fig. 183). He had been a gardener before the war and, as a member of a non-conformist sect

Fig. 184

called the Brethren, thought it wrong to kill, but earned a VC, DCM and Bar, Fig. 185
and MM and Bar. Fig. 184 shows Indian stretcher-bearers at work near
Ginchy on the Somme. The Indian Corps was in France for a year, from late
1914 till late 1915, when it departed for Mesopotamia, but Indian cavalry
remained on the Western Front for the duration of the war. Three of the men
carrying the stretcher are medical assistants by function, but the fourth is a
sowar (trooper) of Indian cavalry, almost certainly the orderly of the British
cavalry officer being carried. In Fig. 185 two Guards Division stretcher-
bearers trudge along the duckboards near Langemarck on the northern end of
the Ypres salient in October 1917.

One of only three men to win the VC and Bar was Captain Noel Chavasse,
RMO of the Liverpool Scottish, who had an MC into the bargain. But in
battle the burden of work at the RAP could overwhelm even the most zealous
doctor, and stretcher-bearers often carried out tasks that went well beyond their

Fig. 186

theoretical competence. Fig. 186 was taken by an official photographer near 'Clapham Junction' on the Menin Road on 26 September 1916, during the battle of Polygon Wood. A sergeant of the Argyll and Sutherland Highlanders, hard hit, is being tended by a stretcher-bearer, his SB brassard just visible. In contrast, Fig. 187 shows an RAP in a gully during the advance of August 1918. The RMO, his position marked by the Red Cross flag, has managed to get most of

Fig. 187

his wounded back to the ADS. In the foreground is a salvage post, where soldiers stack rifles dropped by the dead or discarded by the wounded. Wounded were meant to be disarmed and 'de-bombed' before they left the front line, but even so many appeared at the ADS with live grenades in their pockets.

At the beginning of the war the army concentrated on getting casualties back along the line of medical evacuation as fast as it could. Thanks partly to the advice of some of its civilian consultants, it soon began to push improved medical care closer to the front, so that men could be given more effective treatment sooner after being hit. Fig. 188 shows the walking wounded section of a busy ADS. The man having his leg wound treated has resolutely refused to be parted from his rifle, and a German prisoner (right) looks on. When the Canadian Corps attacked Vimy Ridge in April 1917 its orders affirmed that 'enemy wounded will be treated exactly the same as our own wounded', and though stretcher-bearers would generally pick up friend before foe, the principle was widely observed by both sides. Gas casualties had to be kept separate from others because of the danger of cross-contamination. Fig. 189 (*overleaf*) is supremely evocative, not least because of its remarkable resemblance to

Fig. 188

Fig. 189
(overleaf)

Fig. 190

John Singer Sargent's painting *Gassed*. Taken near Bethune on 10 April 1918 during the battle of the Lys, part of the German spring offensive, it shows men temporarily blinded by mustard gas waiting in their private darkness outside the ADS.

An ADS was run by the static sections of a field ambulance of the Royal Army Medical Corps, whose collecting sections, often using wheeled stretchers, went forward to help regimental bearers bring men back from RAPs. The level of treatment available at the ADS steadily improved, and by 1916 urgent cases could be operated on there, with help from Field Surgical Teams sent up to help with heavy workloads. Even better treatment was available at the Casualty Clearing Station: Fig. 190 shows one of the 'serious' wards at No. 2 CCS at Oursteene near Bailleul in April 1916. From the CCS the wounded man would travel by motor ambulance to a stationary hospital in the rear. On the Western Front men who were badly wounded but fit enough to move were sent to a Loading Station, where they would be placed on a train for the onward journey to Britain. An ambulance train near Doullens in April 1918 is shown in Fig. 191. There is a narrow central aisle, with three tiers of bunks on either side. In contrast, getting men off Gallipoli to the medical

Fig. 191
(opposite)

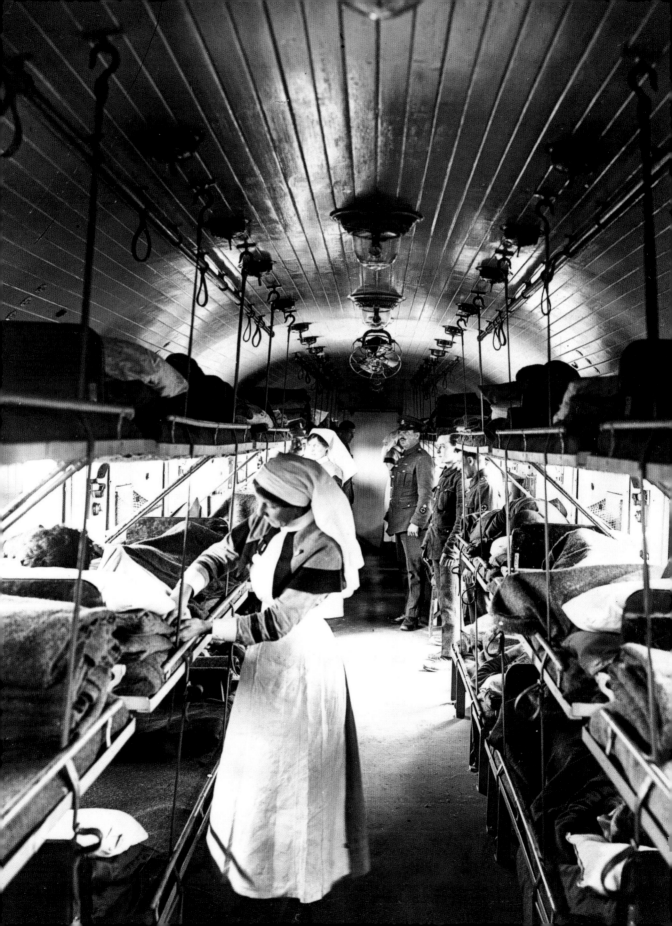

Fig. 192 facilities in Mudros harbour on the island of Lemnos was more problematic. Fig. 192 shows Australian and New Zealand wounded being evacuated from Anzac Cove in April 1915. Walking wounded sit on the steam cutter *Keraunos* (right rear), and there is a lighter packed with stretcher cases on the left.

Some men were killed instantly. Others perished from shock or loss of blood before they could be recovered, and yet others died at a medical facility, or in transit between them. The death rate amongst wounded who reached an ADS was far higher than it would be a generation later, for antibiotics had not yet been discovered, and gangrene remained an ever-present threat. Despite the status accorded to gas and the machine gun by popular mythology, the war's main killer was the shell. Fig. 193 shows two young Highlanders felled by a shell on 21 March 1918. The man on the right has both legs snapped, not by the chunks of spinning metal, but by blast which has flung him backwards faster than bone or joint could sustain. His comrade has been dismembered,

Fig. 193

and it was this sort of butcher's-shop horror, with hot iron reducing the complex and fragile human body to its component parts, that many soldiers found most shocking.

Sometimes the dead were buried with scrabbled informality in the dark behind a trench, or were sent back, often with a carrying party that had brought stores or rations forward, as we see in Fig. 194 (a German photograph in the Imperial War Museum's collections), to be interred with more formality.

Fig. 194

*Fig. 195
(previous
pages)*

In Fig. 195 (*previous pages*) an army chaplain reads the burial service for dead shrouded in blankets or groundsheets. There were times when the sheer scale of the task was beyond the combatants, but in Fig. 196 we see the British burying Turkish dead at Gallipoli, where even across a deep cultural divide there were occasional local truces to allow for common decency.

In 1914 soldiers were issued with a single identity disc, which was retrieved from their body if they were killed so that their death could be recorded. Individuals or small groups buried in isolated graves might easily be lost if the tide of war engulfed their markers, as it so often did, and about 40 per cent of soldiers buried on the Western Front in 1914–15 had no means by which bodies could be identified when small burials were consolidated into bigger cemeteries. By 1916 men were given two discs, so that one could be collected by comrades or even passers-by, and the other left with the body.

Fig. 196

Many men preferred to wear an identity bracelet, and in Fig. 197 a stretcher-

Fig. 197

bearer is removing the bracelet from the body of a Highlander on the edge of a shell-hole. Although soldiers became hardened by the war, they were often sentimental about comrades' graves, going out of their way to maintain them as well as they could.

Fig. 198 is a sight of profound poignancy. The South African Brigade of 9th Scottish Division was badly mauled in Delville Wood. This photograph shows a South African nurse, serving on the Western Front, laying flowers on

Fig. 198

her brother's grave in February 1918, when the wood lay well behind British lines. It was lost and retaken again later that year. We can just make out the name on the cross. Private Douglas Beresford Hoole Fynn of 3rd South African Infantry, of Dohne, Cape Province, was killed on 16 July 1916, and now lies in London Cemetery near Longueval. He was twenty years old.

The term casualties included prisoners of war and soldiers interned in neutral countries. The overall total of prisoners for forces under British command was 192,848, the great majority of them coming from Britain's own regular and reserve forces, with 21 March 1918 the worst single day, with over 21,000 officers and men captured. A man's chance of being taken prisoner hung on several factors. At Gallipoli the Turks found it hard enough to feed their own soldiers, let alone prisoners, some of whom were killed out of hand. And although the garrison of Kut al Amara had its formal surrender accepted, the majority of those captured died of privation and ill-treatment.

On most fronts soldiers on either side would be unlikely to have surrender accepted if they fought to the last extremity, encountered an enemy with a personal or regimental grudge, or had an escort unwilling to take them back through the barrage. Despite well-documented accounts of the murder of prisoners, it is clear that British and Germans alike took prisoners much of the time, and that men who survived the first five minutes of capture were often well treated by men who had been trying to kill them not long before. The German senior NCO who led a successful counter-attack on High Wood in mid-July 1916 marched his prisoners to a field canteen where he bought a bottle of spirits and a big box of cigarettes: he gave all the men a pull at the bottle and a handful of fags apiece before handing them over.

German photographs of British prisoners show all the extremes of reaction: exhaustion, sheer relief, sullenness or defiance. Both sides separated officers from their men immediately after capture, and Fig. 199 shows a column of British officers being escorted to the rear. Their collar-dogs suggest that most are from the same unit, and the fact that several have had time to grab an overcoat implies that this group is the result of the negotiated surrender of one of the redoubts encircled by German stormtroops on 21 March 1918. The officers are in step with one another, though not with their guard.

The men who fought in 1914–18 came from a society which was sub- *Fig. 199*
stantially Christian, with ninety-eight per 1,000 of the population attending
Church of England communion on Easter Sunday in 1911, well over twice
the figure for 1973. Three-quarters of the children in England and Wales went
to Sunday school in 1888. If the majority of soldiers could not have discussed
the doctrine of transubstantiation or the importance of the Synod of Whitby,
most had a fundamental religious belief. One sergeant major told an army
chaplain that 'to most men religion means nothing, except the notion that
there was one above, a sense of duty to live cleanly, and a belief that there
would be a reckoning sometime'. The regimental church parades of pre-war
days, as much military duty as religious ritual, were replaced by a variety of
ceremonies, ranging from large services to tiny gatherings where army padres
or clergymen serving as officers, NCOs or men gave communion in a barn or
dugout.

Fig. 200 Fig. 200 has a significance all of its own, for it is a service just behind the lines on 29 June 1916, at a time when the thud of guns and the wuffle of shells passing overhead must have made it hard for the chaplain to make himself heard. Forty-eight hours later the battle of the Somme would be at fever-pitch, and some of the soldiers in this picture – 17/King's Liverpool (1st Liverpool Pals) – would be dead. The battalion was in 30th Division, recruited largely in Liverpool and Manchester, thanks to the patriotic endeavour of Lord Derby, two of whose brothers commanded an infantry and an artillery brigade in it. The Derby crest was the divisional sign, and the Liverpool Pals wore it as their cap badge: Lord Derby gave a silver badge to every man who had joined before 16 October 1914. Brigadier General the Hon. F.C. Stanley's 89th Brigade was on the right-hand end of the British line, and the commanding officer of 1st Liverpool Pals, Lieutenant Colonel B.C. Fairfax, advanced arm in arm with his French neighbour, Commandant le Petit of 3rd Battalion 153rd Regiment.

Soldiers often judged religion not by the abstractions of its doctrine but by the courage and commitment of its ministers. There were probably as many views on chaplains as there were chaplains in the army, and over 5,000 commissions were given to priests of all denominations during the war. The worst of them stood on their dignity, rarely visited the front, and could not grasp how to combine the task of being both 'Mr God and Mr Cinema', sustaining men's spirits at the same time that they strove to arrange creature comforts. The best struck the balance perfectly, and illuminated all they met by the light of their own belief. Few could equal the Rev. Theodore Bayley Hardy, who joined the army at the age of fifty-four and was awarded the VC, DSO and MC during less than a year in France. Fig. 201 shows him receiving his VC from the King. His daughter, a VAD in France at the time, stands in the background. She had helped him clean his boots the night before the investiture (for, like many of his cloth, he was a little unmilitary), and was always irritated that a painting based on this photograph showed them muddy. This brave and devoted man was mortally wounded trying to bring in wounded just over a month before the war ended: he ran its hazard to the end.

Fig. 201

5

In Parenthesis?

The Armistice with Germany, which came into force at 11 a.m. on 11 November 1918, was the last signed between the Allies and their major opponents: Bulgaria had agreed to a truce on 29 September, Turkey on 30 October and Austria-Hungary on 3 November. Although there was wild rejoicing in London at the news (Fig. 202 shows the scene outside Buckingham

Fig. 202

Fig. 203

Palace), men at the front were often less enthusiastic. Many had never allowed themselves to hope that they would outlast the war, and were stunned by the realisation that they might now live to see their grandchildren. Sometimes their lives were clouded by what we would now call 'survivor guilt'. Fig. 203 shows the transport officer (in a natty British Warm) and two NCOs of the transport section of 4/Worcesters. Sergeant Lester, in the centre, lost a foot on the last day of the war, after thirty years' service. The overwhelming majority of officers and men wanted to get out of uniform, and on with their lives, just as quickly as they could. This was easiest for units in France, though there were small-scale mutinies, best described as soldiers' strikes, by those who felt that the process was simply going too slowly.

In truth, demobilisation presented the authorities with serious challenges. There was now a civil war in Ireland, giving rise to concerns that some Irish soldiers would return home battle-hardened but disaffected, while the young conscripts sent there might not prove reliable. It is easy to forget what the war

Fig. 204

and the Easter Rising of 1916 had done to Ireland. Fig. 204 shows Sergeant Willie Malone, killed with 2/Royal Dublin Fusiliers at Mouse Trap farm during Second Ypres and now commemorated on the Menin Gate. Fig. 205 is his brother Michael, killed fighting against the British in the Easter Rising.

Fig. 206 shows the cricket team from Malahide, in the north of County Dublin, on the eve of war. The tall man on the left is Tom Kettle, Nationalist MP and Professor of National Economics at University College Dublin. Like many of his countrymen, he decided that the cause of Irish nationalism would best be served by helping Britain in her hour of need; he was killed with 9/Dublins at Ginchy in 1916. 'I have mixed much with Englishmen and Protestant Ulstermen,' he wrote in his last letter, 'and know that there is no real or abiding reason for the gulfs, saltier than the sea, that now dismember the natural alliance of both of them with us Irish Nationalists.' A poem dedicated to his daughter Betty concluded:

Fig. 205

Fig. 206

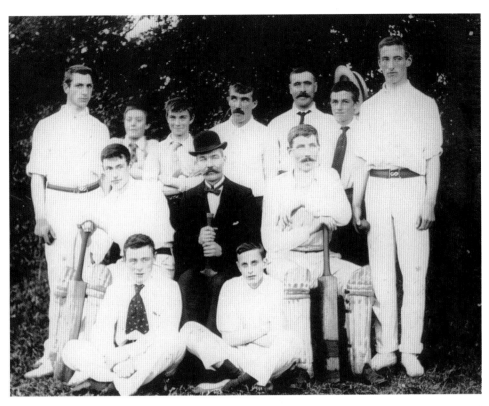

Know that we fools, now with the foolish dead,
Died not for flag, nor King, nor Emperor,
But for a dream, born in a herdsman's shed,
And for the secret Scripture of the poor.

At the other end of the line is Charlie Adams, also a lieutenant in the same battalion, who came back to his cricket at the end of the war, only to find that his comrades who had fought in the British Army were reviled as traitors. Not least amongst the benefits of improved Anglo–Irish relations in the past twenty years has been the rescue of Ireland's Roman Catholic soldiers from historical oblivion: these photographs were supplied by the thriving Royal Dublin Fusiliers Association.

Other military commitments persisted beyond the Armistice. There was a small expeditionary force in north Russia, and a much bigger Army of Occupation, containing some of the best divisions in the army, was dispatched to

Fig. 207 the Rhineland, as we see in Fig. 207, which shows troops marching over the Deutzer Bridge in Cologne. In the right background is the Hohenzollern Bridge: at the height of mobilisation in 1914 troop trains had clattered westwards over it, almost nose to tail. Retrieving troops from India, many of them Territorial units sent there in 1914, was complicated by the fact that there were ongoing

Fig. 208

operations on the North-West Frontier, and in 1919 the Third Afghan War broke out. 1/9th Hampshire, a Southampton-based Territorial cyclist unit, spent most of the war in India: Fig. 208 shows it training for operations in Waziristan. In November 1918 the battalion was sent off to Russia as part of the Siberian Expeditionary Force, reaching Vladivostok at the end of November and Ekaterinburg in May 1919. With the collapse of Allied intervention against the Bolsheviks, the battalion sailed from Vladivostok to Vancouver, crossed Canada by rail, and eventually arrived in Southampton to be disbanded on 5 December 1919.

Fig. 209

Getting soldiers home was difficult enough, and providing the transport required for all their horses and mules was impossible. Most animals in Palestine and Mesopotamia were simply sold to local dealers. Those in France were inspected by the army's vets, and only the best were brought back to Britain. One Royal Welch Fusiliers officer remembered, 'I negotiated for Jenny, the adjutant's hack; but my sentimental gesture fell through as she was graded "for sale on the continent".' Girlie, another of the battalion's horses, was luckier. Duly repatriated, 'She was ridden with the Wynnstay Hounds, and reared a foal which was ridden with the Wynnstay; she lived until 1931.' Many soldiers resented the way that their long-faced chums were cast aside, and paid for last photographs. Fig. 209 shows Private H. Longhurst of the 11th Hussars. The wobbly English of the original caption cannot veil its sentiment:

> **Me & My, Old Pal**
> We landed in France 1914. Served with the Regiment,
> Untill March 11th 1919. —My Pal was sold in
> Belgium on March 12th 1919
> **The Best of old Friend's**
> **must Part.**

A million soldiers of Britain and her Empire would not return home, but lay in formal cemeteries, tiny burial plots or individual graves. Thousands had received no burial at all, but lay where they had fallen, or had been disintegrated by direct hits, climate and carrion. Even marked graves had often been disrupted by shell or mine. Fig. 210 shows soldiers near Ypres in early 1918 washing in a shell-hole edged by grave-markers. The condition of the water does not bear thinking about, still less what must have happened to the bodies beneath it. The large cross between the two crouching figures commemorates Sapper Frank Vickery of 475th Field Company Royal Engineers, killed on 16 August 1917. His parents lived at Westbury on Trym, and his Bristol-raised company was part of 48th South Midland Division. It fought in the battle of Langemarck on 16–18 August 1916, taking the ruined village of St-Julien but being flayed by machine guns as it tried to exploit towards

Fig. 210

Springfield farm. Not surprisingly, Sapper Vickery's grave was lost, and he is now commemorated on the Tyne Cot Memorial on Passchendaele Ridge.

At the end of the war the Imperial War Graves Commission, granted its Royal Charter in May 1917, found itself with some 600,000 burials registered, but another 500,000 bodies were still missing. Some were found very easily. In May 1918 a British corps, battered in the German offensives of March and April, was moved down into the French 6th Army's sector on the Chemin des Dames, where it was duly caught by the May offensive. The photograph in Fig. 211 was published in an American collection (its subject-matter would

Fig. 211

Fig. 212   have been too grim for a British publisher in 1919), and shows a soldier after a year in the open. Other bodies were exhumed from temporary graves or shell-holes as battlefields were combed by search parties made up of Labour Corps soldiers, many of whom had transferred from the infantry at the end of hostilities. In Fig. 212 we see an officer in a mackintosh signing a register held by a sergeant major while the remainder of the party are busy with exhumation. They did what they could to identify bodies, searching necks and wrists for discs or bracelets, and sometimes finding legible papers or an engraved watch, like that which enabled the Australian Second Lieutenant William Putney, killed on 12 October 1917, to be buried in a marked grave in Tyne Cot Cemetery. This, with almost 12,000 graves the largest War Graves Commission cemetery anywhere in the world, was developed from a tiny scattering of graves behind a German bunker used as an aid post. Fig. 213 shows the cemetery in the early 1920s, its consolidation still in progress, and the Commission's standardised wooden crosses. Fig. 214 is a more modern view, with the headstones which replaced crosses in the 1930s. Although the

Fig. 213

photographs are taken from different directions, the German bunker so obvious in the first shot is on the right-hand side of the second, with poplars around it.

Nothing had been done to deal with the dead at Gallipoli after the Allied withdrawal, and the chaotic situation in Turkey at the war's end meant that it was not until 1921 that work could begin. Any qualitative classification of the divisions under British command would place the New Zealand Division near

Fig. 214

Fig. 215

the top of the list: its only failure, in the face of impossible odds, was within sight of Tyne Cot. The New Zealanders are particularly associated with the eminence of Chunuk Bair, where their Gallipoli Memorial to the Missing now stands. In Fig. 215 we see skeletons, many of them those of New Zealanders, collected in groups which strove to give integrity to each set of remains. By the time the photograph in Fig. 216 was taken these relics of humanity had been given individual burials, and the recent photograph in Fig. 217 shows the same

Fig. 216

Fig. 217

site today. The tall pillar is the New Zealand Memorial, inscribed, like similar memorials elsewhere, with the words 'FROM THE UTTERMOST ENDS OF THE EARTH'. The statue to its right is of Lieutenant Colonel Mustapha Kemal (later Kemal Atatürk), who led the counter-attack that pushed the Allies off this crucial ridge.

While the war was still in progress battalions and divisions had begun to commemorate their own triumphs and disasters. Fig. 218 shows a simple memorial to fifty-nine NCOs and men of D Company 2/East Lancashire killed by a single shell on 14 March 1915. Most of the soldiers named on this memorial are now buried in Vieille Chapelle cemetery near Bailleul. Memorialisation was not confined to battlefields. Street memorials had been constructed in Britain during the war, and immediately after it the country

Fig. 218

Fig. 219

was frosted with war memorials in cities, towns and villages, from simple crosses to triumphant tableaux. Let us allow one (though one of the most striking) to speak for all. Charles Sergeant Jagger's Royal Artillery Memorial at Hyde Park Corner commemorates the 49,076 officers and men of the Royal Artillery who died in the war. At its top squats a 9.2-inch howitzer, aimed (should the ballistics of Portland stone permit it to fire) at the Somme. Around it are the massive figures of artillerymen. One of them lies dead, shrouded by his greatcoat, with his helmet placed on his chest. Jagger had joined the Artists' Rifles at the beginning of the war and then been commissioned into the Worcesters. Wounded three times, he had won the MC for gallantry. The highly realistic figures were not to everyone's taste, but Jagger told a newspaper that 'experience of the trenches persuaded me of the necessity for frankness and truth'. The memorial was inaugurated in 1925, and Fig. 219 shows the scene immediately after the opening ceremony.

The thirteen-pounder gun of E Battery Royal Horse Artillery, which had fired the first British shell of the war on the morning of 22 August 1914, was at the ceremony. As we see in Fig. 220, the gun was taken to Hyde Park Corner from the Imperial War Museum, then housed in two galleries in the former Imperial Institute in South Kensington. The museum was reopened on its present site, the former Bethlem Royal Hospital on the Lambeth Road, in 1936. Styled the National War Museum from its foundation in 1917, it adopted its present title in January 1918. It began as a place of commemoration and memorial in itself, and successive changes in its terms of reference have enabled it to include the Second World War, and latterly all conflicts in which Britain and her Commonwealth have been involved since 1914.

The most distinctive commemoration of the war came from an idea by the Reverend David Railton, who had served as a padre on the Western Front and been powerfully moved by the pencilled inscription 'An Unknown British Soldier' on a rough wooden cross. In 1920 he suggested to the Dean of Westminster that an unidentified soldier should be brought back from the battlefield to be buried 'amongst the kings' in Westminster Abbey. Both the Dean and the Prime Minister, David Lloyd George, warmly supported the idea. On the night of 7 November 1920 one body was selected from four flag-draped sets of remains in the chapel at St-Pol near Arras, and was put in *Fig. 220*

Fig. 221

a plain pine coffin, and transferred to the citadel at Boulogne, where a guard of honour of the French 8th Infantry Regiment stood vigil overnight. On the tenth the coffin was enclosed in a mighty casket made from oak trees at Hampton Court Palace, banded with iron, and topped with a medieval sword personally chosen by the King from the royal collection and an iron shield bearing the inscription 'A British Warrior who fell in the Great War 1914–18 for King and Country'. Fig. 221 shows the casket just before it was placed aboard HMS *Verdun* for its journey to Dover.

On the morning of 11 November the casket was drawn on a gun-carriage of the Royal Horse Artillery from Hyde Park Corner, along The Mall to Whitehall, where the cenotaph – a symbolically empty tomb – was unveiled by the King. The Unknown Warrior was then carried between a guard of honour of 100 holders of the Victoria Cross, and laid to rest at the western end of the nave of Westminster Abbey. The guests of honour were a group of about 100 women who had lost their husbands and all their sons in the war. When Lady Elizabeth Bowes-Lyon married the future King George VI in 1926 she laid her bouquet on the tomb on her way into the Abbey, as a tribute to her brother Fergus who had died at Loos in September 1915. All royal brides married in the Abbey have laid their bouquets there on their way back from the altar, and the Queen Mother's own funeral wreath was placed on the tomb there by the present Queen the day after her mother's funeral in 2002.

The burial of the Unknown Warrior, a ritual widely followed in other countries, gave visible expression to a crushing sense of national grief. But it is important to remember that, dreadful though the toll of war dead was, about one in eight of British soldiers who served in the war was actually killed: the majority survived. This figure veils wide statistical variations in the danger of serving at various times on the war's different fronts. On 1 July 1916, for example, the most dangerous arm of the service was the infantry, and the most dangerous rank was captain. About twice as many soldiers had been wounded, in mind or body, as had been killed. Some remained haunted by dark memories, others limped through life with missing limbs, and still others were terribly disfigured. Fig. 222 goes as close to the issue of disfigurement as an official photographer could in showing the result of reconstructive surgery: there were infinitely more shocking sights to be seen on Britain's streets. Here the sculptor Captain Francis Derwent Wood RAMC, who headed the department which made masks for facial wounds at 3rd London General Hospital at Wandsworth, puts the finishing touches to a cosmetic plate to cover a blighted face.

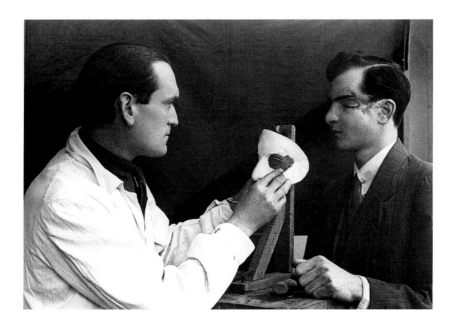

Fig. 222

Fig. 223

Most veterans knew that they were lucky to have survived. David Jones, a private in 15/Royal Welch Fusiliers, dedicated his great poem *In Parenthesis* to 'all common and hidden men . . . and to the enemy front-fighters who shared our pains, against whom we found ourselves by misadventure'. He tells us that the work was so called because 'the war itself was a parenthesis – how glad we thought we were to step outside its brackets at the end of '18'. That is precisely what most veterans did: they got on with their lives. Many lamented the loss of the comradeship which had helped make the struggle bearable, and ex-service organisations, from the British Legion to regimental associations, helped them keep in touch with those with whom they had shared so much. Sometimes they revisited the scenes of their youth. A member of a 17/Royal Fusilier battlefield tour in the early 1930s snapped French labourers on Vimy Ridge reaping that iron harvest which still grows along the Western Front (Fig. 223). More veterans felt that the nation that had been so eager to send them to war did little enough to help them make a living after it. All too often the surprisingly positive tone of letters and diaries actually written during the war is replaced by a note of bitterness as the experience of 1914–18 was seen through the smoky prism of unemployment and the Depression.

This book began by considering the way in which the war was recorded by photographers, professional and amateur. Fig. 224 shows what could so

easily go wrong when an amateur strove to get an 'action' shot. This Lewis *Fig. 224* gun team of 1/5th Essex was photographed not long after the third battle of Gaza in November 1917. The boys are not taking it at all seriously: the gunner has laid down a blanket to protect his elbows, and there is no drum-magazine on the gun. Worse still, the photographer has framed his shot too widely, and in the background, his face obscured by the rim of his steel helmet (these arrived in Palestine a good year after they were common on the Western Front), is a soldier who is definitely not part of the plot. He is 'chatting', removing lice, 'chats' in soldier's slang, and their eggs from the seams of his greyback shirt. To be 'chatty' was to harbour lice, and army-issue longjohns were 'chat bags'. Chatting was an occupation familiar to any front-line soldier, but one which was almost never photographed. The soldier is Private Percy Cook of Black Notley in Essex, who had been wounded in the first battle of Gaza earlier that year. He returned home after the war, and made window-frames for Crittalls for forty-nine years, dying in 1967, when I was an undergraduate, already beginning to write about the events that he, like tens of thousands of his countrymen, had put firmly in parenthesis.

Acknowledgements

The author most gratefully acknowledges the providers of the photographs used in this book, as follows:

Dr Peter Caddick-Adams, Figs 110, 111.

Commonwealth War Graves Commission, Figs 213, 214, 215, 216, 217.

Essex Regiment Museum, Chelmsford, Figs 115, 224.

Finlayson Family Archives, Fig 40.

Mr John Hopkinson, Figs 15, 16, 17, 18, 19.

Horsepower, the Museum of the King's Royal Hussars, Winchester, Figs 90, 91, 92, 93, 94, 209.

The Imperial War Museum, London, Figs 2, 3, 4, 5, 6, 8, 9, 10, 11, 12, 13, 14, 20, 21, 22, 23, 24, 28, 31, 32, 33, 37, 42, 44, 45, 46, 47, 48, 49, 50, 51, 52, 53, 54, 55, 57, 58, 63, 64, 65, 66, 67, 69, 70, 72, 73, 74, 75, 76, 77, 79, 80, 81, 82, 84, 85, 86, 89, 96, 97, 98, 99, 100, 101, 103, 104, 105, 106, 108, 109, 112, 113, 114, 116, 117, 119, 120, 121, 122, 123, 124, 125, 127, 128, 129, 130, 131, 132, 133, 135, 137, 138, 139, 140, 141, 142, 143, 144, 145, 146, 147, 149, 150, 151, 152, 153, 154, 155, 157, 158, 159, 160, 161, 162, 163, 164, 165, 166, 167, 168, 169, 170, 171, 173, 174, 175, 176, 177, 178, 179, 181, 182, 184, 185, 186, 187, 188, 189, 190, 191, 192, 193, 194, 195, 196, 197, 198, 199, 200, 201, 202, 207, 210, 212, 218, 219, 220, 221, 222.

The Liddle Collection, Brotherton Library, University of Leeds, Figs 38, 39, 41, 68, 78, 83, 107, 118, 203.

The Queen's Royal Surrey Regiment Museum, Clandon Park, Fig 34.

The Board of Trustees of the Royal Armouries, Leeds, jacket photograph and Figs 71, 87, 88, 102, 156, 180, 211.

Royal Dublin Fusiliers Regimental Association, Dublin, Figs 204, 205, 206.

Royal Engineers Museum and Library, Chatham, and *The Sapper* magazine of September 1916, Fig 134.

Royal Fusiliers Museum, HM's Tower of London, Figs 29, 136, 223.

Royal Hampshire Regiment Museum, Winchester, Figs 35, 36, 148, 208.

Royal Signals Museum, Blandford, Figs 56, 59, 60, 61, 62.

Staffordshire Regiment Museum, Lichfield, Fig 183.

Mr Ray Westlake for the photographs from his book *The British Army of 1914*, Figs 25, 26, 27, 30, 43, 95.

The photograph of Jackie the baboon in Fig 172 is from Peter Digby's history of 1st South African Infantry Brigade, *Pyramids and Poppies* (Ashanti Publishing, Rivona, Gauteng, Republic of South Africa, 1993). Despite my best efforts I have been unable to make contact with the author.

I owe a particular debt to gratitude to John Yianni of Watercress Photographic who enhanced some of these photographs. Martin Middlebrook and John Dillon both gave me valuable assistance. I was overwhelmed by the kindness and efficiency of most of the museums who provided photographs. It was often the smaller collections, these days so thinly staffed, that did best, usually because they were engaged in what was so evidently a labour of love.